Paul and His Recent Interpreters

Paul

and His Recent Interpreters

E. Earle Ellis

WILLIAM B. EERDMANS PUBLISHING COMPANY
Grand Rapids, Michigan

Library of Congress Catalog Card Number, 61-10853

ISBN 0-8028-1076-4

PHOTOLITHOPRINTED BY CUSHING - MALLOY, INC.
ANN ARBOR, MICHIGAN, UNITED STATES OF AMERICA

PREFACE

It was, I believe, Marcus Dods's remark that the danger of criticism is not what it discovers but that it may turn the student's mind from essentials to minutiae. Critical studies do have a fascination, particularly for the better student, which can result in their becoming an end in themselves. Nevertheless, in today's world historical criticism is a *sine qua non*. Properly applied, it is a valuable tool to uncover the Spirit-carried message of the Scripture.

For seminary students and for others there is a serious need for convenient summaries of research in the various areas of Biblical study. Bible dictionaries, besides being dated, too often are unhelpfully brief or summarize without any interpretation or assessment. The present work seeks to fill this need in some degree in the area of Pauline studies. It is not, of course, the first effort of its kind[1]; and it is by no means comprehensive. It may, however provide a prolegomenon which will make the student of Paul aware of the critical issues and, with that awareness, enable him to measure his exegesis in the light of the critical concerns.

The bibliography in the first chapter is necessarily quite selective. The primary concern has been to choose those works which have set trends or are representative of significant viewpoints. The section on Pauline thought is restricted to the two major foci of twentieth-century studies, *Religionsgeschichte* and eschatology. This approach with its brevity and emphasis upon contrast, is open to criticism. It does serve, however, to accentuate the trends in the research.

The second and third chapters expand upon two specific problems in the area of Pauline thought and Introduction respectively. 'The Structure of Pauline Eschatology' seeks to break new ground in a much debated area. While ever grateful for the many benefits received from the writings of C. H. Dodd, in this matter I am unable to follow the reconstruction which he has popularized for our generation. 'The Authorship of the Pastorals' is purely a summary and evaluation of trends. While indicating my inclinations, it offers no new synthesis. I do not have one. Perhaps the biggest problem of the Pastorals is that each school regards its solution as pat. If the essay broadens that perspective, its purpose will be served.

---

[1] Cf. A. Schweitzer, *Paul and His Interpreters* (London, 1912); A. M. Hunter, *Interpreting the New Testament 1900-1950*, (London, 1951); N. Q. Hamilton, *The Holy Spirit and Eschatology in Paul* (Edinburgh, 1957); W. G. Kümmel, *Das Neue Testament: Geschichte der Erforschung seiner Probleme* (Freiburg, 1958); H. N. Ridderbos, *Paul and Jesus* (Grand Rapids, 1958).

In the preparation of the manuscript I did not have access to Coppens's work on the present state of Pauline studies.[2] Also the important contributions of W. G. Kümmel[3] and H. J. Schoeps[4] came to hand too late to be given the attention they merit. A book of this nature is always an unfinished task. Hopefully, it may provide a few guide lines and, in Pauline eschatology, raise useful questions.

Finally, a word of appreciation is due to the editors of *New Testament Studies, The Evangelical Quarterly, Review and Expositor,* and *The New Bible Dictionary* (forthcoming, London, 1961) in whose pages portions of this material have appeared. Also, I wish to thank Dr. Robert Mounce and Dr. Herman Waetjen, who assisted in the proofreading, and the librarians of Southern Baptist Seminary and Virginia Episcopal Seminary who gave generous accommodations and assistance.

E. EARLE ELLIS

Bethel Seminary
St. Paul, Minn.
1960

[2] J. Coppens, *L'etat present des etudes pauliniennes* (Bruges, 1956).
[3] *Op. cit.*
[4] H. J. Schoeps, *Paulus: Die Theologie des Apostels im Lichte der jüdischen Religionsgeschichte* (Tübingen, 1959; ET: London, 1961).

CONTENTS

ABBREVIATIONS

BJRL   *Bulletin of the John Rylands Library*

CBQ   *Catholic Biblical Quarterly*

DSS   *Dead Sea Scrolls*

ET   *Expository Times*

EusHE   *Eusebius, Ecclesiastical History*

GT   *Gospel of Truth*

HTR   *Harvard Theological Review*

ICC   *International Critical Commentary*

JBL   *Journal of Biblical Literature*

TWNT   *Theologisches Wörterbuch zum Neuen Testament*

NTS   *New Testament Studies*

CHAPTER ONE

PAULINE STUDIES IN RECENT RESEARCH

I. THE LIFE OF PAUL: A SYNOPSIS

Background

From Paul's birth until his appearance in Jerusalem as a persecutor of Christians there is little information concerning his life. Although of the tribe of Benjamin and a zealous member of the Pharisee party,[1] he was born in Tarsus a Roman citizen.[2] Jerome cites a tradition that Paul's forebears were from Galilee. It is not certain whether they (1) migrated to Tarsus for commercial reasons or (2) were colonized by a Syrian ruler. That they were citizens suggests that they had resided there for some time.

William Ramsay and others have shown us that Tarsus truly was 'no mean city'. It was a center of learning, and scholars generally have assumed that Paul became acquainted with various Greek philosophies and religious cults during his youth there. In recent years van Unnik has challenged this assumption.[3] He argues that the relevant texts (Acts xxii. 3, xxvi. 4 f.) place Paul in Jerusalem as a very small child; Acts xxii. 3 is to be read in sequence: (1) born in Tarsus, (2) brought up at my mother's knee (*anatethrammenos*) in this city, (3) educated at the feet of Rabbi Gamaliel. As a 'young man'[4] Paul was given official authority to direct the persecution of Christians and as a member of a synagogue or sanhedrin council 'cast (his) vote against them' (Acts xxvi. 10, RSV). In the light of Paul's education and early prominence we may presume that his family was of some means and of prominent status; his nephew's access to the Jerusalem leaders accords with this impression (Acts xxiii. 16, 20).

Of Paul's personal appearance the canonical account suggests only that it was not impressive (I Cor. ii. 3 f., II Cor. x. 10). A more vivid picture, which Deissmann[5] and Ramsay[6] incline to credit, occurs in the apocryphal 'Acts of Paul and Thecla':

> And he saw Paul coming, a man little of stature, thin haired upon the head, crooked in the legs, of good state of body, with eyebrows joining, and nose somewhat hooked, full of grace: for sometimes he appeared like a man, and sometimes he had the face of an angel.

---

1 Rom. xi. 1; Phil. iii. 5; Acts xxiii. 6.
2 Acts xvi. 37; xxi. 39; xxii. 25 ff.
3 W. C. Van Unnik, *Tarsus of Jerusalem, De Stadt van Paulus' Jeugd* (Amsterdam, 1952).
4 Acts vii. 58; Gal. i. 13; I Cor. xv. 9.
5 A. Deissmann, *Paul* (New York, 1927), p. 58.
6 W. Ramsay, *The Church in the Roman Empire* (London, 1893), pp. 31 f.

Conversion and Early Ministry

While there is no evidence that Paul was acquainted with Jesus during Jesus' earthly ministry,[7] his Christian kinsmen (cf. Rom. xvi. 7) and his experience of the martyrdom of Stephen (Acts viii. 1) must have made an impact upon him. The 'glorified Jesus' question in Acts xxvi. 14 implies as much. The result of Paul's encounter with the risen Christ gives ample assurance that it was an experience of a healthy mind; and it can be adequately interpreted, as indeed Luke does interpret it, only as a miraculous act, which transformed Christ's enemy into his apostle. Acts' three accounts (Acts ix, xxii, xxvi) attest not only to the significance of Paul's conversion for Luke's theme but also, as Munck and others have suggested, to its essential importance for Paul's interpretation (1) of his ministry to the Gentiles and (2) of his union with Christ.

Apart from an interval in the Transjordan desert Paul spent the three years following his baptism preaching in Damascus.[8] Under pressure from the Jews he fled to Jerusalem, where Barnabas ventured to introduce him to leaders of understandably suspicious Christians. His ministry in Jerusalem lasted scarcely two weeks, for again the Jews sought to kill him. To escape, Paul returned to the city of his birth, spending there a 'silent period' of some ten years. No doubt it is silent only to us. Barnabas, hearing of Paul's work and remembering their first meeting, requested him to come to Antioch to help in a flourishing Gentile mission.[9] These newly-named 'Christians' soon began their own missionary work. After a year of notable blessing, Paul and Barnabas were sent on a 'famine visit' to help stricken Christians in Jerusalem.

Mission to Galatia.   The Council of Jerusalem.   Mission to Greece.

Upon their return from Jerusalem — about A.D. 46 — Paul and Barnabas, commissioned by the church in Antioch, embarked upon an evangelistic tour. It took them across the island of Cyprus and through 'South Galatia' (Acts xiii, xiv). Their strategy, which became a pattern for the Pauline missions, was to preach first in the synagogue. Some Jews and Gentile 'God-fearers' accepted the message and became the nucleus for a local assembly. When the mass of Jews rejected the Gospel, sometimes with violence, the focus of the preaching shifted to the Gentiles (cf. Acts xiii. 46 f.). Despite these perils and the defection at Perga of their helper, John Mark, the mission succeeded in establishing a Christian witness in Antioch-Pisidia, Iconium, Lystra, Derbe, and possibly Perga.

In the meantime the influx of Gentiles into the Church raised serious questions concerning their relation to Jewish laws and customs. A number of Jewish Christians were insisting that Gentiles must be circumcised and observe the Mosaic Law if they were to be received 'at par' in the Christian

---

[7] II Cor. v. 16 means only to 'regard from a human point of view'.
[8] Gal. i. 17; Acts ix. 19 ff.
[9] Gal. i. 17 ff.; Acts ix. 26 ff.; xi. 20 ff.

community. Upon his return to Antioch (*c.* A.D. 49), Paul, seeing in this Judaizing movement a threat to the very nature of the gospel, expressed his opposition in no uncertain terms. (1) He rebuked Peter publicly (Gal. ii. 14) after the latter, to avoid a breach with certain Judaizers, had separated himself from Gentile Christians. (2) Hearing that the Judaizing heresy was infecting his recently established churches, Paul wrote a stinging letter of warning to the Galatians in which the Pauline *credo,* 'Salvation by grace through faith', was forcefully presented. These events in Antioch gave rise to the first great theological crisis in the church. To resolve the problems which it raised, the church in Antioch sent Paul and Barnabas to confer with the 'apostles and elders' in Jerusalem (Acts xv). The ensuing council (*c.* A.D. 49-50) gave the judgment that Gentiles should have 'no greater burden' than to abstain from food offered to idols, blood-meat, meat from strangled animals, and unchastity (or incest marriage). The effect of this decision was to sustain Paul's contention that Gentiles were under no obligation to keep the Mosaic Law. The restrictions mentioned seem to have been principally for local application (cf. I Cor. viii) and as an aid to Jewish-Gentile relations.

Because of differences with Barnabas (over taking John Mark along), Paul took a new companion, Silas, on his second missionary tour (*c.* A.D. 50-53; Acts xv. 40 — xviii. 22). From Antioch they travelled overland to the churches of 'South Galatia' and at Lystra added young Timothy to the party. 'Forbidden by the Holy Spirit' to evangelize westward they journeyed northward through 'North Galatia', where some converts may have been made (cf. Acts xvi. 6; xviii. 23). At Troas Paul in a vision saw a 'man of Macedonia' beckoning to him. Thus his evangelization of Greece began. In Macedonia missions were established in Philippi, Thessalonica, and Beroea; in Achaia, or Southern Greece, Athens and Corinth were visited. In the latter city Paul remained almost two years, founding a Christian fellowship that was to be the source of both joy and trial in the future. Through his helpers (Luke the physician joined the party in Troas) and by correspondence (I, II Thessalonians) he also kept in touch with the struggling young churches in Macedonia. The Holy Spirit now moved Paul to turn his eyes once more upon the earlier forbidden province of Asia. Departing Corinth he stopped briefly at Ephesus, the commercial metropolis of Asia, and left as an advance party two Corinthian friends, Priscilla and Aquila. In a quick trip back to Antioch —via Jerusalem — Paul completed his 'second missionary journey' and, after a final sojourn in Antioch, prepared to move his base of operation westward to Ephesus.

The Aegean Ministry

In many ways the Aegean period (*c.* A.D. 53-58; Acts xviii. 23 — xx. 38) was the most important of Paul's life. The province of Asia, so important for the later church, was evangelized; and the Christian outposts in Greece secured. During these years he wrote the Corinthian letters, Romans, and probably the Prison Epistles, which in the providence of God were to constitute a holy and authoritative scripture for all generations. For the Apostle this was a time of triumph and defeat, of gospel proclamation and threatening heresies, of joy and frustration, of activity and prison meditation. The risen Christ used all these things to mold Paul into His image and to speak through Paul His word to the Church.

From Antioch Paul traveled overland through the familiar Galatian region to Ephesus. There he met certain 'disciples' including Apollos, who had known John the Baptist and presumably Jesus (Acts xviii. 24 ff.). On this foundation the Church grew and evangelized the whole province of Asia. God performed such extraordinary miracles that certain Jewish exorcists began, without success, to use the name of 'Jesus whom Paul preaches'. Opposition from devotees of the city's patron goddess, Artemis (Diana), was soon aroused; and Demetrius, a prosperous idol-maker, succeeded (from motives other than piety) in inciting the people to riot. Paul doubtless had made a number of short trips from Ephesus; he took this occasion, some three years after his arrival, to make a final visit to the churches in the Aegean area. Through Troas he came to Macedonia, where he wrote II Corinthians. After a time, he traveled southward to Corinth. There he spent the winter and wrote a letter to the 'Romans' before retracing his steps to Miletus, a port near Ephesus. After a touching farewell, Paul, 'bound in the Spirit' and under threatening clouds, sailed toward Jerusalem and almost certain arrest. These things do not deter him. For Asia has been conquered, and he has visions of Rome.

The Caesarean and Roman Imprisonment. Paul's Death.

Paul disembarked at Caesarea and, with a collection for the poor, arrived at Jerusalem at Pentecost (Acts xxi. 23; cf. I Cor. xvi. 3 f.; II Cor. ix; Rom. xv. 25 ff.). Although he paid his respects to the temple rituals, Jewish pilgrims from Ephesus who remembered 'the Apostle to the Gentiles' accused him of violating the temple and incited the crowds to riot. He was placed under arrest but was permitted to address the crowd and later the Sanhedrin.

To prevent his being lynched, Paul was removed to Caesarea where Felix, the Roman governor, imprisoned him for two years (Acts xxiii — xxvi). At that time Festus, Felix's successor, indicated that he might give Paul to the Jews for trial. Knowing the outcome of such a 'trial', Paul, as a Roman citizen, appealed to Caesar. After a moving interview before the governor and his guests, King Agrippa and Bernice, he was sent under guard to Rome. Thus, under circumstances hardly anticipated, the risen Christ fulfilled the Apostle's dream and His own word to Paul: 'You must bear witness also at Rome' (Acts xxiii. 11, RSV). After a stormy sea-voyage, Paul and his party were wrecked and spent the winter on Malta (c. A.D. 60-61). He reached Rome in the spring and spent the next two years under house arrest, 'teaching about the Lord Jesus Christ quite openly' (Acts xxviii. 31). Here the story of Acts ends, and the rest of Paul's life must be pieced together from other sources.[10]

---

[10] A most helpful survey of the apostolic age, and Paul's place in it, is A. Schlatter, *The Church in the New Testament Period* (London, 1955).

Most probably Paul was released in A.D. 63 and visited Spain and the Aegean area before his re-arrest and death at the hands of Nero (*c.* A.D. 67). The Letter of Clement (v. 5-7; A.D. 95), the Muratorian Canon (*c.* A.D. 170), and the apocryphal (Vercelli) Acts of Peter (i. 3; *c.* A.D. 200) witness to a journey to Spain; and the Pastoral Epistles, or at least II Timothy, involve a post-Acts ministry in the East. To the end Paul fought the good fight, finished the course, kept the faith. His crown awaits (cf. II Tim. iv. 7 f.).

II. THE CHRONOLOGY OF PAUL'S MINISTRY

General Reconstruction

The Book of Acts, augmented with data from the Epistles and from Jewish and secular sources, continues to serve as the chronological framework of Paul's ministry for most scholars. Its sketchiness and chronological vagueness, however, even in those periods treated, is increasingly conceded; and there is a growing willingness to interpolate (e.g., an Ephesian imprisonment) into the framework from other data or reconstructions. Fixed dates with secular history are not numerous. The most certain is the proconsulship of Gallio (cf. Acts xviii. 12), which may be fixed in A.D. 51-52 (Deissmann) or, more probably, A.D. 52-53 (Jackson and Lake, Feine-Behm). If in Acts xviii, 12 Gallio had only recently assumed office (Deissmann), Paul's sojourn in Corinth may be dated between the end of A.D. 50 and autumn A.D. 52. This accords with the 'recent' expulsion of Priscilla and Aquila from Rome (Acts xviii. 2), which probably is to be dated A.D. 50.[11]

Besides the dates above, the mention of King Aretas of Nabatea (II Cor. xi. 32), the famine in Judea (Acts xi. 28), and Paul's trip to Spain and martyrdom in Rome under Nero[12] provide some less specific chronological data. (1) Damascus coins showing Roman occupation are present until A.D. 33, but from A.D. 34-62 they are lacking; this places a *terminus a quo* for Paul's conversion at AD. 31.[13] (2) Josephus notes a severe famine *c.* A.D. 44-48, probably to be located in A.D. 46. (3) From tradition Paul's death may be dated with some probability in the later years of Nero, *c.* A.D. 67.[14] The following outline offers a probable chronology:

Conversion	33
First Visit to Jerusalem	36
(plus 3 years; Gal. i. 18)	
'Famine Visit' to Jerusalem	46
(plus 14 years; Acts xi. 29 f.; Gal. ii. 1)	

[11] The astronomer Gerhardt, following Zahn's exegesis of Acts xx. 6 ff. (that the passover mentioned occurred on a Tuesday), dated that passage in A.D. 58. If so, it would place the accession of Festus (Acts xxiv. 27) in A.D. 60 and give a second firm date. But there are a number of variables which make the calculation only a probability. Cf. P. Feine — J. Behm, *Einleitung in das Neue Testament* (Leipzig, 1950); W. Ramsay, *St. Paul the Traveller and the Roman Citizen* (London, 1895).

[12] Rom. xv. 19; Rev. xviii. 20 (?); I Clement v.; Eus. EH ii. 25 — iii. 1.

[13] I.e., A.D. 34 minus 3; cf. Gal. i. 18; *ICC* on II Cor. xi. 32.

[14] For further detail and alternative reconstructions based upon the above data consult

First Missionary Journey	46-49
Jerusalem Council	50
Second Missionary Journey	Spring 50 — Autumn 52
Aegean Ministry	Spring 53 — Spring 58
(3 years in Ephesus, Acts xx. 31; Summer 56 — Fall 57 in Troas, Macedonia, and Illyricum(?) cf. Rom. xv. 19; Titus iii. 12)	
Caesarean Imprisonment	Summer 58 — Fall 60
House Arrest in Rome	Spring 61 — 63
(Ministry to Spain and the Aegean	63-66)
(Final imprisonment and death in Rome 67)	

The Relation of Acts and Galatians

The only fully satisfying chronology is one in which there is a consensus of Acts, the Epistles, and extra-Biblical sources. One continuing problem for such a synthesis has been the relation between Acts and Galatians. The identification of Paul's visit to Jerusalem in Gal. i. 18, with Acts ix. 26 ff. is seldom questioned: the second visit in Gal. ii. 1 ff. poses the basic problem. Three views are current: Galatians ii equals (1) Acts xv, (2) Acts xi. 27-30, (3) Acts xi and Acts xv. In the past the first view has commanded the largest advocacy[15] and it continues to attract some commentators.[16] The following objections, among others, have combined to undermine it: Galatians ii pictures a second visit and a private meeting without reference to any document; Acts xv is a third visit, one involving a public council and culminating in an official decree. Many scholars regard it as incredible that Galatians would, in a highly relevant context, omit mention of the apostolic council and decree.

The second view, often associated with the South Galatian theory, revives an interpretation of Calvin and removes a number of these objections. Acts xi is (1) a second visit, (2) by revelation, (3) concerned with the poor;[17] the apostolic council in Acts xv occurs after the writing of Galatians and, therefore, is not germane to the problem. Advanced in modern times by Ramsay[18] and recently advocated by Bruce, [19] it is probably the prevailing view among British scholars.[20]

Dissatisfied with both alternatives, most continental writers (e.g., Goguel, Jeremias), followed by a number in Britain and America (e.g., K. Lake, A. D. Nock), regard Acts xi and Acts xv as duplicate accounts of Galatians ii, which Luke, utilizing two sources, failed to merge.[21] Against Ramsay, Lake urges that if the Judaizing problem is settled in Acts xi (= Gal. ii), Acts xv is

Feine — Behm.

15 Cf. J. B. Lightfoot, *Epistle to the Galatians* (London, 1892), pp. 123 f.; E. de W. Burton, *The Epistle to the Galatians* (Edinburgh, 1921), pp. 115 f.

16 Cf. H. Schlier, *An die Galater* (Göttingen, 1951), pp. 66 ff.; H. Ridderbos, *Galatians* (Grand Rapids, 1953), pp. 34 f.

17 Cf. Gal. ii. 1, 2, 10.

18 *Traveller*, pp. 54 ff.

19 F. F. Bruce, *The Acts of the Apostles: Greek Text* (London, 1951), pp. 31 f.

20 C. S. C. Williams, *The Acts of the Apostles* (New York, 1957), pp. 22 ff.

21 Cf. E. Haenchen, *Die Apostelgeschichte* (Göttingen, 1956), pp. 57 f., 328.

superfluous. Gal. ii. 9, however, pictures not a settlement but only a private, tacit approval of Paul's gospel and is incidental to the purpose of the visit which, as Lake admits, is the 'care of the poor.'[22] Haenchen (p. 328) rejects Ramsay's 'crucial' application of Galatians ii. 10 to the famine visit. He may be correct in identifying the 'poor' with the Gentile mission (Gal. ii. 9), but it scarcely has the vital significance which he attributes to it. Ramsay's reconstruction, even with some exegetical gnats, remains the more probable alternative. Basically, the view identifying Acts xi and Acts xv arises from (1) the traditional equation of Galatians ii and Acts xv and (2) an excessively negative estimate of Luke's acquaintance with and interpretation of the primary sources. When Galatians ii = Acts xi provides 'a perfectly clear historical development,' [23] it is unnecessarily complex.[24]

A New Reconstruction

Convinced that the Acts framework is unreliable, John Knox[25] offers an imaginative chronological reconstruction from the evidence of the letters. A fourteen-year 'silent period' (A.D. 33-47) is impossible; therefore, the apostle's missionary activities (and some letters) are largely to be placed between his first (A.D. 38; Gal. i 18) and second (A.D. 51; Gal. ii = Acts xv) visits to Jerusalem. The final tour ends with his 'collection visit' and arrest (A.D. 51-53; Rom. xv. 25; I Cor. xvi. 3 f.). Why a silent period (which means simply that it yields no extant letters and did not fit Luke's theme) is so impossible is not readily apparent; and the traditional equation of Acts xv and Gal. ii also is open to question. Knox's fertile mind has found here more admirers than followers, for 'it is difficult to exchange tradition with imagination (as we find it in Acts) for imagination (however reasonable) without tradition'.[26]

III. INTRODUCTION

Early Developments

In a brilliant historical survey Albert Schweitzer[27] traces the development of critical studies in Germany following the Reformation. For the orthodox, Scripture sometimes was little more than a mine of creedal proof texts; exegesis became the servant of dogma. The eighteenth century witnessed a reaction by pietists and rationalists who, each for his own purpose, sought to

---

22 F. J. Foakes–Jackson, and K. Lake, ed., *The Beginnings of Christianity* (London, 1933), V, 201 f.

23 W. L. Knox, *The Acts of the Apostles* (Cambridge, 1948), p. 49; A. S. Geyser, 'Paul, the Apostolic Decree and the Liberals in Corinth', *Studia Paulina, Festschrift* for J. de Zwaan (Haarlem, 1953), pp. 124-38.

24 Other views of the problem are expressed by T. W. Manson (*BJRL*, 24, 1940, pp. 58-80), who identifies Gal. 2 with a visit prior to Acts xi, and M. Dibelius, whose excessive *tendenz* criticism absolves both Acts xi and Acts xv of any claim to historicity. M. Dibelius, *Studies in the Acts of the Apostles* (London, 1956), pp. 100 f.

25 J. Knox, *Chapters in a Life of Paul* (Nashville, 1950), pp. 74-88.

26 W. D. Davies, 'Paul', *Twentieth Century Encyclopedia* (Grand Rapids, 1955), pp. 854-6.

27 A. Schweitzer, *Paul and his Interpreters* (London, 1912); cf. also P. Feine, *Der Apostel Paulus* (Gütersloh, 1927), pp. 11-206.

distinguish exegesis from creedal conclusions. Philological exegesis and the interpretation of Scripture by Scripture became normative for scientific interpretation.

This development finds perhaps its most important expression in J. S. Semler, who, with J. D. Michaelis, pioneered the development of literary-historical criticism. His 'Prolegomena' to theological hermeneutics, 'Paraphrases' of Romans and Corinthians, and other writings emphasize that the New Testament is a temporally conditioned document in which the purely cultural references are to be distinguished and/or eliminated. Philology exists to serve historical criticism. Our copies of Paul's letters have a 'church liturgy' format and must, then, face the possibility that they originally had a different form. Specifically, Semler suggests that Rom. xv and xvi; II Cor. ix; xii. 14 — xiii. 14 were separate documents, later incorporated into the larger epistles. Foreshadowing the conclusions of F. C. Baur, Semler contrasts Paul's non-Jewish ideas with the Jewish-Christian party whom the Apostle opposed; the General Epistles reflect an effort to mediate this conflict.

The Tübingen School

In nineteenth-century Germany exegesis was fully transformed from the 'servant of dogma' to the 'servant of scientific philosophy'.[28] In Pauline studies a trend appeared in J. E. C. Schmidt (1805) who, on literary grounds, doubted the authenticity of I Timothy and II Thessalonians. Schleiermacher (1807), Eichhorn (1812), and DeWette (1826) brought II Timothy, Titus, and Ephesians also under question. After Baur's thoroughgoing scythe only five of the twenty-seven New Testament documents remained uncontested witnesses from the apostolic period. Apart from Revelation, all were Paul's (Romans, Corinthians, Galatians).

F. C. Baur of Tübingen was not content merely to test the authenticity of ancient documents, a common practice since the Renaissance. His was a 'positive criticism' which sought to find the documents' true historical setting and meaning. In Symbolik und Mythologie, the book which brought about his faculty appointment, he revealed the set of his mind and of his future work with the declaration that 'without philosophy history seems to me dumb and dead'.[29] Baur's philosopher was Hegel, and his history was the apostolic Church. To apply the Hegelian dialectic, which viewed all historical movement as a series of theses (advance), antitheses (reaction), and syntheses (= a new thesis), Baur needed an interpretive key. He found it in I Cor. i. 12: conflict between Paul, the apostle to the Greeks (advance), and the narrow Jewish Christianity of the original disciples (reaction) was the clue to the history of the apostolic age. Only under the threat of Gnosticism was Catholic unity (synthesis) achieved in the late second century. In this 'tendency criticism' all New Testament writings which 'tended' toward compromise between Paul and the original apostles were viewed as later attempts

---

28 Cf. G. W. Bromiley, Biblical Criticism (London, 1948). C. W. Dugmore, ed., The Interpretation of the Bible (London, 1944), pp. 92—107.

29 Cf. S. M. Jackson, ed., Schaff-Herzog Encyclopedia (New York, 1908), II, 7 f.

at unity through rewriting history. The then current literary analysis of Paul's letters favoured Baur's reconstruction and, in turn, the latter accentuated and confirmed the suspicions of the more extreme literary critics. The Tübingen School rapidly became the dominant factor in New Testament criticism.

Using Baur's logic and sparked by Bruno Bauer's commentary on Acts (1850), an ultra-radical school questioned the genuineness of all Pauline literature: (1) Acts knows no Pauline letters, and its simple picture of the Apostle may be more primitive than the letters; disagreements even within Romans and Galatians suggest several hands and a later time. (2) If Pauline thought (Paulinism) is the Hellenization of Christianity, as Baur thought, is it possible that this was accomplished so quickly and by one man? Could anti-Jewish feeling or Paul's high Christology have developed in a Palestinian-based Church so soon after Jesus' death? No, the conflict itself is the climax of a long development, and Paulinism is to be identified with a second-century Gnostic party who used the Apostle's 'letters' as an authoritative vehicle for their own ideas. Why letters? Because apostolic letters already had a position of authority. Why Paul? This is impossible to say.

For all their logic the radicals succeeded only in convincing themselves. The citation of Paul by I Clement (A.D. 95) and Ignatius (A.D. 110), and the neglect of Paulinism and lack of anti-Jewish conflict in the post-apostolic literature were fatal to their argument. The omission in Acts of Pauline literary activity was a (not very strong) argument from silence. The net effect of the 'Ultra-Tübingen School' was to undermine Tübingen itself. For, within their common assumption that Paul was the Hellenizer of Christianity and that Hegel supplied the key to history, the radicals had the better argument.

Baur's views came under attack from the conservatives (e.g., J. C. K. von Hofmann) and the followers of Schleiermacher (e.g., Ewald); perhaps the cruelest and most telling blow was from A. Ritschl, a former disciple. Both Ritschl and von Hofmann rejected the alleged hostility between Paul and the original disciples. The latter's emphasis upon the unity of apostolic teaching was in the next century to find renewed expression in the writings of P. Feine and A. Schlatter and in the kerygmatic theology of C. H. Dodd. A moderating literary criticism, even among Baur's disciples (e.g., Pfleiderer), revised the estimate of genuine Pauline epistles sharply upward. Apart from the Pastorals the majority of critics excluded only II Thessalonians and Ephesians, and even the acceptance (e.g., by Harnack and Julicher) of these latter two was no longer a mark of conservatism. With its literary and philosophical presuppositions undermined, the influence of Tübingen waned. Nevertheless, in three ways its impact was decisive for biblical studies. (1) By tying literary analysis to an imaginative philosophical synthesis, Baur, whom Godet called Semler *redivivus,* dominated New Testament criticism (as Semler never did) for half a century. (2) Although his own exegesis proved to have a philosophical bias unacceptable to later historians (and to all committed to a theistic interpretation of history), Baur brought into prominence an inductive historical approach to earliest Christianity and freed research from a tradition which came to much of the data with its conclusions already assumed. For this, all students can appreciate his labors. (3) Finally, because Baur's reconstruction placed in bold relief the problems facing historians of the apostolic age, he largely set the course of future studies. What was the relationship between Paul and Jesus? What was the influence of Jewish and Hellenistic thought in the apostolic Church? What are the proper philosophical presuppositions for a study of Christian origins? The Tübingen school died, and today there is no apparent sign of a resurrection.[30] But the forces which gave it birth continued fecund and, for a corpse, even Tübingen retained a remarkable familiarity with the following generations.

British Contributions in the Nineteenth Century

British (and American) scholars interacted with the Tübingen reconstruction but, with one or two exceptions (e.g., S. Davidson), they did not find it persuasive. Likewise, the Pauline corpus (minus Hebrews) continued to find acceptance. In America some rejected the Pastorals (e.g., B. W. Bacon, A.C. McGiffert) ; Britain, following J. B. Lightfoot,[31] generally accepted them in a post-Acts setting. Nevertheless, with characteristic *Vorsichtigkeit*, British scholars influenced future criticism, more than is generally realized, by solid historical exegesis (e.g., Lightfoot, Ramsay) and by relating Paul to contemporary Jewish thought (e.g., F. W. Farrar, H. St. J. Thackeray). William Ramsay's[32] espousal of the Lukan authorship of Acts after thoroughgoing archaeological and historical research was particularly influential for the critical reconstruction of Paul's life.[33] With the advocacy of Harnack and Deissman[34] this conclusion has been strengthened, although some recent students[35] have argued anew against the tradition.

Trends in the Twentieth Century

Literary criticism in the present century has focused upon (1) a continuing effort toward a general historical reconstruction,[36] (2) the publication of the Pauline corpus, (3) the provenance and date of the Prison Epistles, and (4) authorship and other questions concerning individual epistles.

In spite of the demise of the Tübingen school, its historical reconstruction and some of its literary foibles have continued to be assumed in much contemporary critical study. Johannes Munck has rightly objected that when the literary conjectures failed, the dependent historical conjectures ought to

---

30 Its recent airing in S. G. F. Brandon's *The Fall of Jerusalem and the Christian Church* (London, 1951) does not appear to have imparted life.

31 J. B. Lightfoot, *Biblical Essays* (London, 1904), pp. 397-410.

32 Cf. *Traveller*, pp. 20 ff.

33 W. K. Hobart's conclusions regarding *The Medical Language of St. Luke* (Dublin, 1882) also remain, with qualifications, a valid contribution in this area.

34 Deissmann, *op. cit.*, p. 26.

35 E.g., Haenchen, *op. cit.*

36 Cf. also 'Pauline Thought', *infra*.

have been revised.[37] Munck himself proposes such a revision. (1) The Jerusalem church, i.e., the original disciples, even as Paul, had no interest in excluding or 'judaizing' Gentiles. (2) It was Paul's conviction, and his sole difference with the Jerusalem church, that Gentiles must *first* be won. Thus, as *the* Apostle to the Gentiles (Gal. ii. 7) he restrains Antichrist (II Thess. ii. 7), and by evangelism brings in (representatively) the 'fullness of the Gentiles' (Rom. xi. 25; xv. 19). As a decisive eschatological act, Paul initiates Israel's redemption by making her jealous (Rom. xi. 11) in taking the 'Gentile' collection to Jerusalem (Acts xx. 4; I Cor. xvi. 3). Israel's 'No' issues in Paul's arrest and death but, as Jesus, Paul dies knowing God will yet answer that 'No' in the fullness of time. In interpreting Paul's ministry within the framework of his initial call and of his eschatology, Munck gives due heed to critical emphases; on balance, his work marks a constructive advance.

E. J. Goodspeed,[38] departing from Harnack and earlier authorities, drew fresh attention to the formation of the Pauline corpus. He conjectured that about A.D. 90 an admirer of Paul in Ephesus published the Apostle's letters (excepting the Pastorals) and wrote Ephesians himself as an 'Introduction'. J. Knox[39] took the hypothesis a step further and identified that admirer with the slave, and later bishop of Ephesus, Onesimus. While receiving considerable acceptance,[40] the theory has been unpersuasive to many. (1) The text demands some addressee; and the primitive omission of one points to a circular letter, hardly suitable for a corpus introduction. (2) Ephesians never introduces or ends the Pauline corpus in any ancient MS. (3) It is very doubtful that the content of Ephesians can be properly described as a non-Pauline summation of Pauline thought. (4) G. Zuntz,[41] while recognizing the possibility of earlier pre-corpus collections in Ephesus, finds that the textual and other evidence points rather to *c.* A.D. 100 and to 'the scholarly Alexandrian methods of editorship'.

The provenance of Paul's prison letters has been a matter of increasing interest since G. S. Duncan, following Lisko and Deissmann, located them in *St. Paul's Ephesian Ministry.*[42] Although Acts mentions no Ephesian imprisonment, Paul's letters imply it;[43] also the setting, journeys, and personages of the prison letters fit Ephesus better than distant Rome.[44] J. Knox,[45] Michaelis[46] and, as to Philippians, F. F. Bruce[47] and T. W. Manson[48] are

---

[37] J. Munck, *Paul and the Salvation of Mankind* (Richmond, 1960), pp. 70-77: 'It was not enough merely to transfer the problem from the two centuries to the three decades' (p. 70).
[38] E. J. Goodspeed, *The Meaning of Ephesians* (Chicago, 1933).
[39] J. Knox, *Philemon Among the Letters of Paul* (Nashville, 1959), pp. 98 ff.
[40] Cf. C. L. Mitton, *The Formation of the Pauline Corpus of Letters* (London, 1955).
[41] G. Zuntz, *The Text of the Epistles* (London, 1953), pp. 14 ff., 276-9.
[42] A Caesarean provenance has few advocates today.
[43] E.g., I Cor. xv. 32; II Cor. i. 8; vi. 5; xi. 23.
[44] Cf. Philemon 22; Phil. ii. 24 with Rom. xv. 24 ff.; *NTS, III* (1956-57), 211-218.
[45] *Philemon*, p. 33.
[46] W. Michaelis, *Einleitung in das Neue Testament* (Bern, 1954), pp. 205 ff., 220.
[47] Bruce, *op. cit.,* p. 341.
[48] *BJRL,* 22 (1939), 182 ff.

sympathetic to Duncan. C. H. Dodd[49] and Percy[50] object that (1) the tradition apart from Marcion's Prologue is unanimous for Rome, and such
probably (though not certainly) is the meaning of Phil. iv. 22; (2) such references as I Cor. xv. 32 are to be taken metaphorically; (3) the 'developed
theology' of the captivity epistles suggests the later Roman date. On balance,
the Ephesian provenance is inviting and, at least in the case of Philippians,
may prove to be a permanent advance.

At the beginning of the century some attention was given to interpolation
criticism, a kind of New Testament Wellhausenism, which sought to distinguish Pauline and other hands according to style and/or subject matter. The
arbitrary selection of criteria caused Schweitzer[51] to remark that one scholar's
'Pauline' core had a suspicious resemblance to the Good Friday meditations
of his *Christian Century*. While such criticism generally has been rejected,
fragment hypotheses still are applied to II Corinthians and the Pastorals.
Using more objective criteria derived from the nature and practice of ancient
letter writing, Otto Roller[52] gives a verdict of genuine to all thirteen Pauline
letters. Roller's important work illustrates the considerable shift in the
climate of scholarship since Deissmann,[53] some fifty years ago, felt it necessary
to rebuke the delusion 'that a Biblical scholar's scientific reliability is to be
assessed according to the number of his critical verdicts of "not genuine".'

Concerning individual letters, critical emphases have shifted, except in the
case of Ephesians and the Pastorals, from authorship to other matters. Many
British and American scholars favor an early date for Galatians (*c.* A.D. 49,
from Antioch) and a South Galatia destination, i.e., to the churches founded
on Paul's first mission tour. Continental scholars favor North Galatia, i.e.,
the ethnic region (Acts xvi. 6; xviii. 23), and a post-Acts xv chronology. The
order of I and II Thessalonians is reversed by T. W. Manson; and differences
of style and subject matter cause Harnack to suppose that II Thessalonians
was written to the Jewish Christians.[54] Munck,[55] following Cullmann, identifies the restraining power in II Thess. ii. 6 f. with Paul himself. The Corinthian correspondence includes, in addition to the canonical epistles, a letter
prior to I Corinthians and a 'painful letter',[56] which are identified by some
scholars with II Cor. vi. 14 — vii. 1 and II Cor. x — xiii respectively. R. G. V.
Tasker[57] argues for the unity of our second epistle. A more plausible case
for the combination of two letters occurs in Romans; there the concluding
doxology occurs after xiv. 23 and xv. 33 in a number of MSS., and the addressee
in Rom. i. 7, 15 is missing in a few. Of several explanations the one given

49 C. H. Dodd, *New Testament Studies* (New York, 1953), pp. 85-108.
50 E. Percy, *Probleme der Kolosser-und Epheserbriefe* (Lund, 1946), pp. 473 f.
51 Schweitzer, *op. cit.*, p. 147.
52 O. Roller, *Das Formular der paulinischen Briefe* (Stuttgart, 1933).
53 Deissmann, *op. cit.*, pp. 15 f.
54 Cf. Davies, *op. cit.*
55 Munck, *op cit.*, pp. 36 ff.; but see L. Morris, *The First and Second Epistles to the Thessalonians* (Grand Rapids, 1959), pp. 219 ff.
56 Cf. II Cor. ii. 4; vii. 8.
57 R. V. G. Tasker, *Second Corinthians* (Grand Rapids, 1958), pp. 15-35.

by T. W. Manson,[58] among others, is most attractive: Rom. i — xv was a circular letter to which chapter xvi, an introduction of Phoebe to the Ephesians, was attached in the Ephesus copy. Nevertheless, the traditional view continues to find wide support.[59]

A 'circular letter' appears to be indicated in the case of Ephesians by the currency of the practice in the first century[60] and the necessity for, and yet manuscript omission of, an addressee. Such a view militates against Goodspeed's corpus introduction theory, but it leaves open Sanders' view[61] that Ephesians is not an epistle but Paul's 'spiritual testament'. It also might explain the title 'to the Laodiceans' which, according to Tertullian, Marcion gave the letter.[62] E. Percy[63] has given the most recent argument for the Pauline authorship; C. L. Mitton[64] argues against it. A more popular 'pro and con' is found in F. L. Cross's symposium, *Studies in Ephesians*.[65] 'Which is more likely,' asks H. J. Cadbury,[66] 'that an imitator of Paul in the first century composed a writing ninety or ninety-five percent in accordance with Paul's style or that Paul himself wrote a letter diverging five or ten percent from his usual style?' With the increased tendency to allow for variation in Pauline literary and theological expression the arguments against genuineness have become less compelling; they are weakened further by the Dead Sea Scroll parallels.[67]

Most students consider the nineteenth-century 'non-Pauline' verdicts valid only for the Pastorals.[68] Anglo-American opinion has followed P. N. Harrison's[69] 'fragment hypothesis', i.e., Pauline fragments supplemented and edited; most Continentals who reject the Pastorals favor, with Dibelius,[70] a later Paulinist author. The case for genuineness has found support in Roller's 'secretary hypothesis', i.e., that stylistic variations stem from Paul's amanuensis,[71] the traditional view has been argued anew by Spicq and Michaelis.[72] Growing dissatisfaction with Harrison's hypothesis, as expressed in Guthrie,[73] Michaelis, and Metzger,[74] may forecast a general reappraisal of the prevailing view.[75]

[58] *BJRL* 31 (1948), 224-40.
[59] Cf. Davies, *op. cit.*
[60] Cf. Zuntz, *op. cit.*, p. 228.
[61] Cf. F. L. Cross, *Studies in Ephesians* (London, 1956), pp. 15 ff.
[62] Cf. Col. iv. 16.
[63] Percy, *op. cit.*
[64] C. L. Mitton, *The Epistle to the Ephesians* (Oxford, 1951).
[65] Cross, *op. cit.*
[66] *NTS*, V (1958-59), p. 101.
[67] D. Flusser, 'The DSS and Pre-Pauline Christianity', *Aspects of the DSS*, ed., C. Rabin and Y. Yadin (Jerusalem, 1958), p. 263.
[68] In recent years Pauline *Authorship of the Epistle to the Hebrews* (London, 1939) has been seriously argued only by the Roman Catholic scholar William Leonard.
[69] P. N. Harrison, *The Problem of the Pastoral Epistles* (London, 1921).
[70] M. Dibelius, *Die Pastoralbriefe* (Tübingen, 1931).
[71] So J. Jeremias, *Die Briefe an Timotheus und Titus* (Göttingen, 1947); Feine-Behm. *op. cit.*
[72] Spicq, *op. cit.*; Michaelis, *op. cit.*
[73] D. Guthrie, *The Pastoral Epistles* (Grand Rapids, 1957).
[74] *Expository Times*, LXX (1958-59), 91 ff.
[75] Cf. *infra*, pp. 49-57.

IV. PAULINE THOUGHT

Background

The Reformation emphasis upon righteousness or 'justification by faith' (Rom. i. 17) continued to be in the following centuries the controlling factor in the interpretation of Paul's doctrine. With the rise of literary criticism the absence of this motif became sufficient reason to suspect or even reject a 'Pauline' letter; and in the incipient development of Paulinism, i.e., the system of Pauline thought, 'righteousness' was regarded as the key to the Apostle's mind.[76]

L. Usteri (1824) and A. F. Daehne (1835) sought to explain the whole of Pauline thought in terms of the imputed righteousness of Rom. iii. 21 ff. In contrast, the rationalist H. E. G. Paulus, starting from texts that stress the 'new creation' and sanctification,[77] insisted that Pauline righteousness was an ethical, moral concept; faith in Jesus meant ultimately the faith of Jesus. These two ideas and their relationship had a continuing significance throughout the nineteenth century.

F. C. Baur, within the framework of Hegelian idealism, sought at first (1845) to explain Paul the Hellenizer in terms of the Spirit given through union with Christ by faith. Later, however, Baur reverts to the Reformation pattern, a compartmentalized presentation of the various Pauline doctrines without any attempt to view them from a unified concept. This *loci* approach was followed by succeeding writers who gave minute descriptions of Pauline doctrine, innocently supposing 'that in the description they possessed at the same time an explanation'.[78]

Nevertheless, some writers pressed toward the discovery of a unifying concept for Pauline thought. R. A. Lipsius (1853) recognized two views of redemption in Paul, the juridical (justification) and the ethical ('new creation'). Herman Lüdemann, investigating *The Anthropology of the Apostle Paul* (1872), concluded that the two views of redemption actually rested on two views of the nature of man. In Paul's earlier 'Jewish' view (Galatians; Rom. i — iv) redemption was a juridical verdict of acquittal; for the mature Paul (Rom. v — viii) it was an ethical-physical transformation from 'flesh' to 'spirit' through communion with the Holy Spirit. The source of the first idea was Christ's death; the second, his resurrection. On the other hand Richard Kabisch argued that Pauline redemption essentially meant deliverance from coming judgment, and its significance, therefore, was to be found in the *Eschatology of Paul* (1893). The Christian must walk in newness of life to show that he actually shared Christ's resurrection. 'Spiritual' life and death in the modern religious sense are unknown to Paul; both concepts are, e.g.,

---

[76] In the following sketch compare especially Schweitzer, *op. cit.* More recently cf. R. Bultmann's articles in *Theologische Rundschau* 1 (1929), 26-59; 6 (1934), 229-46; 8 (1936), 1-22; H. N. Ridderbos, *Paul and Jesus* (Grand Rapids, 1958), pp. 3-20; W. G. Kümmel, *Das Neue Testament, passim.* See also B. M. Metzger, *Index to Periodical Literature on the Apostle Paul* (Leiden and Grand Rapids, 1960).

[77] E.g., II Cor. v. 17; Rom. viii. 29.

[78] Schweitzer, *op. cit.*, p. 36.

in Rom. vi, always physical, and the new life is a mystical union with Christ. Thus future deliverance from Satanic powers is anticipated by the possession of the Holy Spirit, who manifests the new age in the present and inseminates our corporal being with a super-earthly substance.

For both Lüdemann and Kabisch, (1) Paul's doctrine of redemption emanates from one fundamental concept. (2) It is a physical redemption to be understood in terms of Pauline anthropology. (3) To be redeemed means to share Christ's death and resurrection, which involves union with Christ and the abolition of the 'flesh'. (4) Although future, this redemption is mediated in the present by the Holy Spirit.

But questions remained. In what sense can Christ's death and resurrection be repeated in the believer? In what sense can the Christian be 'a new creation' and yet outwardly appear unchanged? Albert Schweitzer,[79] building upon the interpretations of Lüdemann and Kabisch, sought an answer in the following synthesis. (1) Paul, as did Jesus, interpreted Jesus' death and resurrection to be eschatological, i.e, an end of the world event, bringing the Kingdom of God and the resurrection life to all the elect. (2) But the world did not end, and believers did not in fact enter into resurrection life; in time the temporal separation between Christ's resurrection and the (anticipated) resurrection of believers became the chief problem for Paul's teaching. (3) To answer it Paul posited a 'physical mysticism': through the sacraments the Holy Spirit mediates in the present time Christ's resurrection to the 'last generation' believers. (4) This present union with Christ in the Spirit ensures to the believer a share in the 'messianic resurrection' at the parousia.

Thus, Schweitzer set the stage for twentieth-century discussions of Pauline eschatology. It was his great merit (1) that he sought to understand Paul's thought in terms of one fundamental concept, (2) that he recognized the central importance of eschatology and (Jewish) anthropology in the Apostle's doctrine of redemption, and (3) that he recognized the Holy Spirit and the *en Christō* union as the realization of the new age in the present. But Schweitzer's interpretation of Paul's eschatology as a makeshift expedient (and as a sacramental mysticism) is questionable. For, as Hamilton's critique has pointed out,[80] the exalted Christ, not the 'delay' in the parousia, determined Paul's eschatology. Also, if Paul's thought patterns are Jewish (as Schweitzer rightly recognized), sacramental mysticism is a rather awkward explanation of the realism of the 'new creation' in Christ.

In addition to eschatology as the key to Paulinism, a closely related question important for the future also had its rise in the nineteenth century: are Paul's thought patterns Jewish or Hellenistic? Kabisch and Schweitzer insisted that Pauline thought was Jewish to the core. Others, following F. C. Baur's reconstruction of Paul as the 'Hellenizer of Christianity', interpreted Pauline anthropology and eschatology from the standpoint of a modified Hellenistic dualism. The antithesis between 'flesh' and 'spirit' in Romans

---

[79] Schweitzer, *op. cit.*

[80] N. Q. Hamilton, *The Holy Spirit and Eschatology in Paul* (Edinburgh, 1957), pp. 50 ff.

vi — viii is an ethical dualism, and 'dying' and 'rising' a spiritual transformation. This has its roots in an anthropological dualism; thus, in the future, redemption involves the deliverance of the 'soul' from its house of clay. But Paul also speaks of the resurrection of the whole man from death (I Thess. iv; I Cor. xv). Otto Pfleiderer[81] concluded that Paul held Jewish and Greek views simultaneously, 'side by side, without any thought of their essential inconsistency.' In interpreting Pauline eschatology elsewhere[82] he posited a development from I Thess. iv through I Cor. xv to II Cor. v. The first is simply Jewish resurrection eschatology; in II Cor. v the believer goes to the heavenly realms at death.

The Origin of Paul's Religion: Hellenism

Twentieth-century studies of Pauline thought have devoted themselves primarily to three questions. What is the relation between Paul and Jesus? What are the sources for Pauline thought? What is the role of eschatology in the mind of Paul?

The distinction raised a half century earlier between 'juridical' (Rom. i—iv) and 'ethical' (Rom. v — viii) righteousness bore much fruit; and the latter, with its 'in Christ' emphasis, came to be regarded as the more central and decisive Pauline concept. A. Deissmann[83] viewed 'in Christ' as an intimate spiritual communion with Christ, a Christ mysticism; more often the 'mysticism' was interpreted as a sacramental reality based upon Jewish eschatology (Schweitzer) or the Hellenistic mysteries.[84] Somewhat later J. S. Stewart (*A Man in Christ* [London, 1935], p. 150 ff.) reflected this trend in British scholarship, regarding union with Christ as the central element in Paul's thought. This emphasis has had important consequences for the course of Pauline studies in the twentieth century.

The contrast between the 'liberal Jesus' and Paul's indwelling, and yet transcendent, Christ called forth at the turn of the century a spate of books on the relationship of Jesus and Paul.[85] W. Wrede's influential *Paulus*[86] put the matter in starkest terms: Paul was not truly a disciple of Jesus; he was actually the second founder of Christianity. The individual piety and future salvation of the rabbi Jesus had been transformed by the theologian Paul into a present redemption through the death and resurrection of a christ-god. Paul's ideas could not, of course, be accepted at face value. To do so would, as Weinel[87] remarked, 'stifle the claims of reason for the sake of Christianity, for reason is forever repeating... that the modern conception of the world is the right one.' Nevertheless, the historian's task remained. If Paul's doctrines did not arise from and build upon the mind of Jesus, what was their origin?

---

81 O. Pfleiderer, *Paulinism* (London, 1891), p. 264.
82 Cf. Schweitzer, *op. cit.*, pp. 70 f.
83 Deissmann, *op. cit.*, pp. 148 ff.
84 Cf. J. Weiss, *Earliest Christianity* (New York, 1959 [1937]), II, 463 f.
85 Cf. Feine, *Paulus*, pp. 158 ff.
86 Tübingen, 1905.
87 H. Weinel, *St. Paul* (London, 1906), p. 11.

F. C. Baur sought to explain the mind of Paul in the context of church controversy: Paul was the champion of Gentile freedom. For Schweitzer the origin of Paul's thought was his peculiar eschatological problem forged in the mental cauldron of late Judaism. The rising History of Religion *(Religionsgeschichte)* school however, found no evidence to ground Paul's sacramental mysticism in Judaism. While recognizing the eschatological problem, it built upon Baur's 'Gentile' Paul and developed still another elaborate reconstruction of the apostolic age. Represented most notably by R. Reitzenstein and W. Bousset,[88] it interpreted Paulinism in the framework of oriental-hellenistic mystery religions. As did Paul, the Mysteries spoke of a dying-rising god, of 'Lord', of sacramental redemption, of 'mysteries', 'gnosis', and 'spirit'. As a boy in Tarsus and later as a missionary the Apostle came under the influence of these ideas, and they exerted a profound influence on his theology. A. Schweitzer,[89] H. A. A. Kennedy[90] and J. G. Machen[91] subjected this reconstruction to a thorough critique, pointing out that in ignoring the Old Testament-Judaism background of the parallels (which Kennedy showed to be quite plausible) and the late date of its sources, the theory reflected a weakness in methodology. The principle contribution of the History of Religion school was to raise the important question of Paul's theological relation to the Gentile religious world. The 'mystery religion' reconstruction did not win wide approval, but in a more recent gnostic dress its general outlines continue today to be strongly advocated.

The mystery religion parallels paled; nevertheless, the conviction remained strong that Paul's thought was substantially Hellenistic. R. Bultmann[92] pointed to the affinity of Paul's literary style with the Stoic diatribe. Others regarded Paul's doctrine of the 'corporate body',[93] his natural theology in Romans i (cf. Acts xvii), and his concept of conscience[94] to be rooted in Stoicism. The inadequacy of these conclusions was urged, respectively, by E. Best,[95] B. Gaertner[96] and C. A. Pierce.[97] Gaertner argues that Paul's 'natural theology' is thoroughly Old Testament-Jewish; however, Pierce concludes that the New Testament adopts in the case of 'conscience' a general Hellenistic usage.

To determine the relationship of Paul to Hellenistic thought the area currently receiving most attention is Gnosticism. This religious-philosophical

---

[88] R. Reitzenstein, *Die hellenistischen Mysterienreligionen* (Leipzig. 1927); W. Bousset,
[89] Schweitzer, *op. cit.*, pp. 179-236.
Kyrios Christos (Göttingen, 1913).
[90] H. A. A. Kennedy, *St. Paul and the Mystery Religions* (London, 1913). Cf. R. E. Brown, 'The Semitic Origin of the Pauline *Mysterion*', Dissertation, John Hopkins University, 1958; cf. *Biblica* 39 (1958), 426-48; 40 (1959), 70-87; *CBQ* 20 (1958), 417-43.
[91] J. G. Machen, *The Origin of Paul's Religion* (Grand Rapids, 1947 [1925]), pp. 255-90.
[92] R. Bultmann, *Der Stil der paulinischen Predigt und die kynisch-stoische Diatribe* (Göttingen, 1910).
[93] Cf. W. L. Knox, *St. Paul and the Church of the Gentiles* (Cambridge, 1939).
[94] E. Norden, *Agnostos Theos* (Leipzig, 1913).
[95] E. Best, *One Body in Christ* (London, 1955), pp. 83 ff.
[96] B. Gaertner, *The Areopagus Speech and Natural Revelation* (Uppsala, 1955), p. 133-69.
[97] C. A. Pierce, *Conscience in the New Testament* (London, 1955), pp. 16 ff., 22 ff., 57 ff.

movement stressed (1) a matter/spirit dualism, (2) deliverance from 'matter' through a divine gift and power of *gnosis,* i.e., a special *knowledge* of God, and (3) mediating angels to assist one to salvation. Long ago J. B. Lightfoot[98] detected elements of Gnosticism in the Colossian heresy. Early in the twentieth century Bousset and J. Weiss[99] urged that aspects of Paul's own thought lay in this direction. Rudolf Bultmann (with his 'school') is the chief representative and developer of Bousset's reconstruction today.

From existentialist considerations Bultmann again makes 'justification' a central Pauline motif, although it is far from a return to Baur or to the Reformers; for the same reasons Paul's anthropology is given a thorough exposition.[100] But the real clue to Bultmann's understanding of Paulinism is his grounding of Pauline thought in Hellenistic Judaism and Hellenistic Christianity. From this background Paul obtained a number of concepts, e.g., sacramental redemption and ethical dualism, which were Gnostic or gnosticized in some degree.[101] While Paul opposed the Gnostics, e.g., at Colossae, in the process he modified not only his terminology but also his concepts, particularly his Christology (Messiah Jesus becomes a heavenly Lord; cf. Bousset) and cosmogony (the demon controlled world is redeemed by a heavenly man).[102]

Schweitzer[103] predicted that a hellenized Paulinism was a half-way house which would have to carry its conclusions to the genesis of Christianity. His prediction was more than fulfilled by the discovery of the Dead Sea Scrolls with their ethical dualism and emphasis on 'knowledge'. The Dead Sea Scrolls are an embarrassment for Bultmann's reconstruction, for 'pre-Gnostic' is about the closest identification most scholars care to make for them. Also, there is little reason to believe that Paul reflects, e.g., 'an earlier Gnostic doctrine about the descent of a redeemer, especially since there is no evidence that such a doctrine existed.'[104] Almost all else that Bultmann chooses to refer to Gnostic influence likewise suffers from the same chronological strictures. R. M. Grant, looking back to Schweitzer, interprets Gnosticism as arising from a failure of the apocalyptic hope; unlike Schweitzer he views Paul as a man whose spiritual world lies somewhere between Jewish apocalyptic and the fully developed Gnosticism of the second century (p. 158). Grant sees the latter tendency in Paul's interpretation of Christ's resurrection as a realized (eschatological) victory over the cosmic powers.[105] More cautiously, R. McL. Wilson, in a valuable assessment of *The Gnostic Problem,*[106] concludes that Paul adopts a Hellenistic cosmogony and terminology only to oppose Gnos-

98 J. B. Lightfoot, *Colossians and Philemon* (London, 1886), pp. 71-111.

99 Cf. Weiss, *op. cit.,* II, 650 f.

100 R. Bultmann, *Theology of the New Testament* (London, 1952), I, 190-227.

101 Bultmann, *op. cit.,* pp. 63 ff., 124 ff., 151-188; cf. 'Gnosis', *Bible Key Words,* II, ed. J. R. Coates (New York, 1958).

102 Cf. W. L. Knox, *Gentiles,* pp. 220 ff. But see G. B. Caird, *Principalities and Powers* (Oxford, 1956); *Theologisches Wörterbuch zum Neuen Testament,* II, 568-70.

103 Schweitzer, *op. cit.,* p. 231.

104 R. M. Grant, *Gnosticism and Early Christianity* (New York, 1959), p. 69; Cf. pp. 39-69. Cullman (in JBL 74, 213-26; ET 71, 9 ff.), calling DSS 'gnostic', uses the term much too broadly. Cf. R. McL. Wilson, *The Gnostic Problem* (London, 1958), pp. 73 ff.

105 *Op. cit.,* p. 158.

106 *Op. cit.,* pp. 75-80, 108, 261.

ticism and to interpret Jesus' authority over the (Gnostic) 'powers'; the Apostle rejects the gnosticizing interpretation.[107]

All the 'Greek' reconstructions of Paul have their root in F. C. Baur's interpretation of Paul as the exponent of Gentile Christianity. When W. Wrede and others recognized the redemptive-eschatological character of Pauline thought, the Apostle was set in opposition not only to Jewish Christianity but to the liberal Jesus himself. But, as Schweitzer had shown, the liberal Jesus was not the Jesus of the Gospels. Bultmann[108] accepted Schweitzer's 'apocalyptic' Jesus but insisted that God's demand for man's decision, not the apocalyptic window-dressing, was the essence of Jesus' eschatology. The suffering, resurrected, and returning Son of Man was a 'mythologized' picture of the later Hellenistic Christology. The mind of Paul remained far distant from the mind of the earthly Jesus or of his earliest disciples. One's estimate of Paulinism is closely tied, therefore, to one's estimate of the Gospel picture of Jesus.

A number of mediating scholars, taking their cue from Bernhard Weiss, see 'development' as the key to Paul's thought. In view of fading parousia hopes, Paul's anthropology and eschatology move toward a Greek dualism (Dodd) and his cosmogony moves toward Gnosticism (R. M. Grant).

In its present *religionsgeschichtliche* format the Hellenistic school is subject to a number of criticisms. There is a tendency to convert parallels into influences and influences into sources. And some of the 'sources' for Pauline thought come from a period considerably later than the Apostle's lifetime. (Bultmann's Paul may have more than a casual relation to the Gnostic 'Paul' of the Ultra-Tübingen School.) Also, its historical inquiry sometimes has been compromised by an inadequate world-view.[109]

Perhaps the most basic questions are these: Is Paulinism best understood as an amalgam, gathered here and there, or as the expansion and application of a central tradition rooted in the mind of Jesus Christ and the earliest Church? Is Paul's mind most adequately explained within a Hellenistic syncretism or within the bosom of Palestinian Judaism and the primitive Church? Does the Hellenization of Christianity begin in Paul and pre-Pauline Christianity (Bultmann) or in Paul's Gentile disciples; and does it arise from a failure of the primitive eschatology in Paul (Grant) or from a misunderstanding of it in his churches?

The Origin of Paul's Religion: Judaism

Both Ritschl and von Hofmann had argued, *contra* Baur, for the unity of Paul's teaching with that of the earliest Church. A. Resch,[110] in the 'Jesus or Paul' debate, upheld this view. But could not rather Paul be the source of

---

[107] However, J. Dupont (*Gnosis: La connaissance religieuse dans les Épitres de saint Paul* [Paris, 1949]) argues that Pauline *gnosis* is strictly Old Testament-Jewish.

[108] Bultmann, *op. cit.*, pp. 23, 30 ff.

[109] For example, Bultmann, like Weinel, views the natural world as a 'self-subsistent unity immune from the interference of supernatural powers' (*Kerygma and Myth*, ed. H. W. Bartsch [London, 1953], p. 7; cf. pp. 5-8, 216, 222;) Cf. Hamilton, pp. 71-82.

[110] His thorough investigation of *Der Paulinismus und Die Logia Jesu* (Leipzig, 1904), concluded that the words of Jesus were a primary source of Pauline thought.

the Synoptic Jesus? The research of several recent writers has substantiated the priority argued by Resch. C. H. Dodd[111] established that a *kerygma,* i.e., a gospel-core proclamation, underlay both the Gospels and Paul, 'a tradition coeval with the Church itself'. The same writer,[112] building upon Rendel Harris's *Testimonies,*[113] found a 'substructure of New Testament theology' to which Paul was indebted and whose origin pointed to Christ himself. E. E. Ellis, examining the hermeneutical principles of *Paul's Use of the Old Testament,*[114] suggested that some common (pre-Pauline) exegetical tradition originated with 'prophets' of the earliest Church. E. Lohmeyer[115] interpreted Phil. ii. 5 ff., with its exalted *kurios* Christology, as a primitive Christian hymn probably arising in Aramaic circles. Similarly, the pre-Pauline character of *The Primitive Christian Catechism*[116] was demonstrated by P. Carrington.

O. Cullmann,[117] K. H. Rengsdorf,[118] and H. Riesenfeld[119] point to a rationale for this understanding of Christian origins. The New Testament concept of apostle has its origin in the rabbinic *shaliah,* an authorized agent equivalent to the sender himself. The apostles witnessed to a tradition or *paradosis* given to them by Christ. 'But since everything has not been revealed to each individual apostle, each one must first pass on his testimony to another (Gal. i. 18; I Cor. xv. 11), and only the entire *paradosis,* to which all the apostles contribute, constitutes the *paradosis* of Christ.'[120] Thus, as an 'apostle' Paul's message is defined in terms of what he has received: his catechesis, kerygma, and the wider 'tradition' would be, and critical study finds them to be, rooted in the earliest Church and ultimately in the teaching of Jesus. And this teaching of Jesus seems to have been not merely moral instruction or apocalyptic warning but creative, theological synthesis which envisioned a post-resurrection ministry by his disciples.[121] In view of these studies (to say nothing of J. Munck's recent thesis)[122] the dichotomy between Paul and the primitive Jewish church, which has been urged from Baur to Bultmann, must be carefully reappraised.

To understand a writer it would seem to be proper to give priority to that milieu to which he appeals and to which he presumably belongs. In interpreting Pauline concepts it is not the categories of a second-century Hellenistic

---

111 C. H. Dodd, *The Apostolic Preaching and its Development* (London, 1936), p. 56.

112 C. H. Dodd, *According to the Scriptures* (London, 1952), pp. 108 ff.

113 Cambridge, 2 Vols. 1916, 1920.

114 Edinburgh and Grand Rapids, 1957; pp. 97 f., 107-12.

115 E. Lohmeyer, *Kyrios Jesus* (Heidelberg, 1928); E. G. Selwyn, *First Epistle of St. Peter* (London, 1946), pp. 365-9, 458-66. Cf. Ridderbos, *op. cit.,* pp. 80-9; R. P. Martin, *An Early Christian Confession* (London, 1960), pp. 8-16.

116 Cambridge, 1940.

117 O. Cullmann, 'The Tradition', *The Early Church* (London, 1956), pp. 60-99.

118 K. H. Rengsdorf, 'Apostleship' in *Bible Key Words,* II, ed. J. R. Coates (New York, 1958).

119 H. Riesenfeld, *The Gospel Tradition and Its Beginnings* (London, 1957). Cf. *CBQ* 22 (1960), 416-21.

120 Cullmann, *op. cit.,* p. 73.

121 Cf. J. Jeremias, *Jesus' Promise to the Nations* (London, 1958), pp. 71 ff.; R. H. Fuller, *The Mission and Achievement of Jesus* (London, 1954), pp. 118 ff.

122 Munck, *op. cit.*

Gnosticism (however easily they may be read back),[123] but the categories of first-century rabbinic/apocalyptic Judaism which demand first claim upon the critical historian's mind.

The nature of first-century Judaism is complex, and it is easy to overdraw or wrongly define the contrast between the 'Hellenized' and the 'Old Testament-Jewish' (terms not necessarily to be equated with *'diaspora'* and 'Palestinian').[124] Nevertheless, considerable research relates the thought of Paul, the Pharisee and 'Hebrew of the Hebrews',[125] with Palestinian rabbinism and apocalypticism rather than with a Hellenized *diaspora.* Van Unnik[126] has raised at least the probability that Paul's early youth was passed not in Tarsus but in Jerusalem. Certainly Paul used the Septuagint and preached among the *diaspora,* and he could employ Hellenistic religious terminology. He may have been acquainted with the syncretistic Judaism exemplified by Philo; but with the doubtful exception of the Wisdom of Solomon, his relationship to the *diaspora* literature is not direct and probably reflects only tradition which both had in common.[127] His more direct relationships lie in another direction. W. D. Davies, in a significant work, has demonstrated that the relation of *Paul and Rabbinic Judaism*[128] forms the background of many Pauline concepts formerly labeled Hellenistic. The Dead Sea scrolls have also confirmed in remarkable fashion the Jewishness of Pauline and New Testament backgrounds.[129]

Passing to specific Pauline concepts, anthropology and the nature of the 'in Christ' relationship have had a central importance since the days of F. C. Baur. It is widely recognized today that Paul views man in an Old Testament-Jewish framework and not in the Platonic dualism of the Hellenistic world.[130] The corporate 'body of Christ' also is best understood not in terms of a Gnostic mythology (Käsemann) nor a Stoic metaphor (W. L. Knox) but as the Old Testament-Jewish concept of corporate solidarity.[131] Davies[132] has related Paul's thought here to the rabbinic speculations on the body of Adam. J. A. T. Robinson's *The Body*[133] correctly finds Paul's ultimate rationale in the

[123] In the light of *Newly Discovered Gnostic Writings* (W. C. van Unnik, London, 1960, p. 93) such reconstructions no longer can be so easily made.

[124] Cf. Acts vi. 1; W. D. Davies, *Paul and Rabbinic Judaism* (London, 1955), pp. 1-8. Schoeps (*op. cit.,* pp. 25f.) finds in both *diaspora* and Palestinian Judaism diverse streams, libertine and orthodox, assimilationist and Zionistic. The degree to which various strata of first-century Judaism had assimilated Hellenistic thought-forms is a basic and continuing problem.

[125] Phil. iii. 5.

[126] Van Unnik, *Tarsus; supra,* p. 11.

[127] Cf. Ellis, *Testament,* pp. 76-84.

[128] Davies, *op. cit.*

[129] K. Stendahl, ed., *The Scrolls and the New Testament* (New York, 1957), pp. 94-113, 157-82; F. F. Bruce, *Biblical Exegesis in the Qumran Texts* (Grand Rapids, 1959), pp. 66-77; Flusser, *op. cit.;* S. E. Johnson, 'Paul and the Manual of Discipline,' *HTR,* XLVIII (1955), 157-65.

[130] Bultmann, *Theology,* I, 209 f.; O. Cullmann, *Immortality of the Soul or Resurrection of the Dead?* (London, 1958), pp. 28-39; J. A. T. Robinson, *The Body* (London, 1952).

[131] E. Käsemann, *Leib und Leib Christi* (Tübingen, 1933); W. L. Knox, *Gentiles,* p. 161.

[132] Davies, *Judaism,* pp. 53 ff.

[133] London, 1952.

realism of Semitic thought patterns, as they are applied to Messiah and his people.[134] E. Best,[135] in viewing the concept metaphorically, falls short of this realism.[136]

Whether Paul's eschatology is rooted in Jewish or Greek concepts is a matter of continuing debate. The importance of this question for Paulinism requires that some detailed attention now be given to it.

The Eschatological Essence of Pauline Thought

C. A. A. Scott's well written *Christianity According to Saint Paul*,[137] over against Albert Schweitzer's eschatological interpretation, identifies salvation as the fundamental concept of Paulinism. But what is the factor determining the character of Paul's 'already but not yet' redemption theology? Not grasping Schweitzer's basic question, Scott does not really pose an alternative: he found a motif to describe Paul, not a key to explain him.[138] Schweitzer may not have stated the problem, or the solution, satisfactorily; but his identification of the key concept remains valid.

Until recently, discussion of New Testament eschatology revolved about the views of Schweitzer and C. H. Dodd.[139] Schweitzer argued that Paul's *en Christo* concept arose from the failure of the Kingdom of God, i.e., the end of the world, to arrive at Christ's death and resurrection. Against Schweitzer, Dodd contended that in Christ's death the 'age to come' did arrive; eschatology was 'realized' as much as it ever would be in history. The believer already participates in the Kingdom (e.g., Col. i. 13), and at death he fully enters the eternal, i.e., eschatological, realm. Eschatology, therefore, does not refer to an end-of-the-world event; in Platonic fashion it is to be understood in non-temporal terms, eternity over against time. How then is Paul's anticipation of a future parousia to be accounted for? Believing it to be a hangover from apocalyptic Judaism (and quite alien to the central message of Jesus), Dodd goes back to Pfleiderer for an answer: in I Thess. iv. Paul has a strictly Jewish eschatology but in I Cor. xv modifies it with the concept of a 'spiritual' body; II Cor. v., which places the believer in heaven at death, expresses the view of the mature (and 'Greek') Paul.[140]

It is Dodd's great merit that he saw, as Schweitzer did not, the essential im-

---

134 Cf. Ellis, *Testament,* p. 136.; R. P. Shedd, *Man in Community* (London, 1958).

135 Best, *op. cit.,* pp. 83-95, 112.

136 Cf. also the essays of K. Barth, *Christ and Adam* (New York, 1956), and J. Murray, *The Imputation of Adam's Sin* (Grand Rapids, 1959); D. R. G. Owen in *Body and Soul* (Philadelphia, 1956) offers an illuminating comparison of Biblical anthropology with the modern scientific view of man.

137 Cambridge, 1927.

138 Cf. also recent Christological approaches, e.g., L. Cerfaux, *Christ in the Theology of St. Paul* (New York, 1959).

139 For Bultmann, eschatology has nothing to do with the future or with history; it is the realm of existential living. Like F. C. Baur, Bultmann uses New Testament language to clothe an imposing philosophy of religion; exegesis becomes the servant of existentialism. Cf. N. Q. Hamilton's *The Holy Spirit and Eschatology in Paul,* pp. 41-90, for a lucid summation and critique of the eschatology of Schweitzer, Dodd, and Bultmann.

140 J. A. T. Robinson's *Jesus and His Coming* (London, 1958, pp. 160 ff.) is essentially an elaboration of Dodd's thesis.

portance for New Testament thought (and for the relevance of the gospel in the present age) of the 'realized' aspect of the Kingdom of God. But in adopting an unbiblical 'Greek' view of time Dodd failed to do justice to the futurist and temporal character of eschatological redemption. Also, a development (i.e., Hellenization) of Pauline eschatology involves an un-Pauline anthropological dualism and, in part, reflects a misunderstanding of the texts. Both Schweitzer and Dodd made admirable attempts to achieve a comprehensive interpretation of New Testament eschatology. Although 'futurist or realized' has now been recognized (correctly, we may believe) as an improper either/or, the contributions of Schweitzer and Dodd remain fundamental landmarks in the progress of the research.

The important monographs of W. G. Kümmel[141] argue convincingly that both 'present' and 'future' eschatology are equally and permanently rooted in the teaching of Jesus and of Paul. Oscar Cullmann's most significant publication, *Christ and Time*,[142] contrasts the Greek idea of redemption, i.e., to escape the time 'circle' at death, with the biblical concept that redemption is tied to resurrection in future 'linear' time, i.e., the parousia. These works, plus a proper appreciation of Paul's Old Testament-Jewish anthropology and of the Semitic concept of corporate solidarity, form a proper foundation for understanding Paul's eschatology — and thus his total doctrine of redemption.

Historical research since the Reformation has recognized that Pauline theology is above all a theology of redemption. The nineteenth century witnessed a growing emphasis upon the present 'union with Christ' (rather than imputed righteousness) as the central aspect of this redemption. Since Albert Schweitzer two eschatological *foci*, Christ's death and resurrection and the parousia, have been pointed to as the key to the meaning of 'union with Christ'.[143]

Jesus Christ in his death and resurrection defeated for all time the 'powers' of the old aeon — sin, death, and the demonic 'rulers of this darkness'.[144] In 30 A.D. Christians were crucified, resurrected, glorified, and placed at God's right hand with Christ.[145] 'In Christ' Christians have entered the resurrection age; the solidarity with the first Adam in sin and death has been replaced by the solidarity with the eschatological Adam in righteousness and immortal life.

This corporate redemption in and with Jesus Christ, this 'new age' reality, which the believer enters at conversion,[146] finds an individual actualization in the present and the future. In the present life it means a transformation through the indwelling Spirit, the first fruits of the new resurrection life,[147]

---

141 W. G. Kümmel, *Promise and Fulfillment* (London, 1957), pp. 141-55; cf. *NTS*, V, 1958-59, pp. 113-26.
142 London, 1951.
143 While 'in Christ' is the basis and sphere of 'juridical' righteousness, the latter (as well as how one becomes 'in Christ') remains a significant part of Paul's thought.
144 Eph. vi. 12; Col. ii. 15.
145 Gal. ii. 20; Eph. ii. 5 f.
146 Cf. Rom. vi.
147 Rom. viii. 23; II Cor. v. 5.

of one's ethic,[148] and of one's total world view.[149] However, in the midst of moral-psychological renewal the Christian remains, in his mortality, under the death claims of the old age. But this too is to be understood no longer in terms of 'in Adam', but as a part of the 'in Christ' reality; for 'the sufferings of Christ abound to us',[150] and the Christian dead have fallen asleep 'in Jesus'.[151] The individual actualization of Christ's sufferings is, of course, in no wise a self-redemption process; rather, it means to be identified with Christ 'in the likeness of his death'.[152] The 'likeness of his resurrection' awaits its actualization at the parousia when the individual Christian, raised to immortal life, 'shall be conformed to the image of His Son, that he might be the first born among many brethren'.[153]

Thus, Pauline redemption is not a 'spiritual' deliverance culminating in the escape of the 'soul' at death (Dodd); it is a physical redemption culminating in the deliverance of the whole man at the parousia (Cullmann). It is to be understood not in terms of a Greek dualism but in the framework of the Old Testament-Jewish view of man as a unified being and as one who lives not only as an individual but in 'corporate solidarities'. The future that has become present in the resurrection of Jesus Christ is a future which the Christian realizes now only corporately, as the 'body of Christ'. However, at the parousia faith shall become sight, 'away' shall become 'at home', and the solidarities of the new age shall become individually actualized in all their glory. This is the living hope of Paul's heart; and in it one finds the meaning of his theology.

148 Col. ii. 20; iii. 1, 9 f., 12.
149 Rom. xii. 1 ff.
150 II Cor. i. 5; cf. Phil. iii. 10; Col. i. 24.
151 I Thess. iv. 14; cf. Phil. ii. 17; II Tim. iv. 6.
152 Rom. vi. 5.
153 Rom. viii. 29; cf. I Cor. xv. 53 ff.

CHAPTER TWO

THE STRUCTURE OF PAULINE ESCHATOLOGY
(II Corinthians v. 1-10)

Since the days of Pfleiderer[1] II Cor. v. 1–10 has been commonly regarded as showing a hellenization of Paul's eschatology, or in today's language, a transition from a futurist to a realized (or inaugurated) eschatology.[2] Paul's earliest view (I Thess. iv. 13 ff.) followed the ancient Jewish idea of physical resurrection at the last day; in I Cor. xv this is qualified by distinguishing between the σῶμα ψυχικόν and the σῶμα πνευματικόν; II Cor. v completes the process, viewing the transition in Greek fashion as occurring at death rather than at the parousia. Although W. D. Davies locates 'the two diverse strains in Paul's conception of resurrection' in (a hellenized) Judaism, the end result is the same: in contrast to I Cor. xv 'resurrection' in II Cor. v takes place at death.[3] Some writers, following Pfleiderer, have contended that Paul, for a shorter or longer period, held both Jewish and Greek concepts 'without any thought of their essential inconsistency'.[4] Even scholars normally opposed to a Greek dualism in Pauline anthropology tend toward it when interpreting II Cor. v. 8. Thus, J. A. T. Robinson is content to equate 'absent from the body' with the 'naked' interim state.[5] Also Cullmann, who has emphasized the temporal character of redemption focused upon the parousia, refers this verse to Paul's confidence concerning the intermediate state.[6]

[1] Cf. A. Schweitzer, *Paul and His Interpreters* (London, 1912), pp. 69–76.

[2] Cf. R. H. Charles, *The Doctrine of a Future Life* (London, 1913), pp. 437 ff.; A. Plummer, *Second Corinthians*, Edinburgh, 1915, p. 153; H. Windisch, *Der Zweite Korintherbrief* (Göttingen, 1924), p. 157; H. W. Robinson, *The Christian Doctrine of Man* (Edinburgh, 1926), p. 130; H. L. Goudge, *Second Corinthians* (London, 1927), pp. 45 ff.; W. L. Knox, *St Paul and the Church of the Gentiles* (Cambridge, 1939), pp. 128 ff.; J. Lowe, 'An Examination of Attempts to Detect Developments in Paul's Theology', *J. Theol. Stud.* XLII (1941), pp. 129 ff.; H. A. Guy, *The New Testament Doctrine of the 'Last Things'* (London, 1948), p. 117; W. H. P. Hatch, 'St Paul's View of the Future Life', *Paulus Hellas-Oikumene* (Athens, 1951), p. 96; R. Bultmann, *New Testament Theology* (1952), II, 201; J. Dupont, ΣΥΝ ΧΡΙΣΤΩΙ, *L'Union avec le Christ suivant Saint Paul* (Paris, 1952), C. H. Dodd, *New Test. Stud.* (Manchester, 1953), pp. 109 ff.; R. F. Hettlinger, '2 Corinthians 5. 1–10', *Scottish J. Theol.* x (1957), 174 ff.; J. A. T. Robinson, *Jesus and His Coming* (London, 1957), pp. 101, 160 f.

[3] W. D. Davies, *St Paul and Rabbinic Judaism* (London, 1955), p. 319; cf. Charles, *op. cit.* p. 453. Hettlinger (*op. cit.* p. 192) takes the unusual view that II Cor. v represented only a temporary aberration caused by recent afflictions (II Cor. i. 8–9); in Philippians (iv. 6) Paul returns to his parousia hope.

[4] O. Pfleiderer, *Paulinism* (London, 1891), I, 264; cf. Lowe, *op. cit.* p. 142: '[Paul] left the whole wonderful muddle unarranged and alive.' This view, however, for which 'from the whole range of the history of thought no analogy could be produced', has been unsatisfactory to most. Schweitzer, *op. cit.* p. 77.   [5] J. A. T. Robinson, *The Body* (London, 1952), pp. 17, 29, 77.

[6] O. Cullmann, *Christ and Time* (London, 1951), pp. 238 ff.; *Immortality of the Soul or Resurrection of the Dead* (New York, 1958), pp. 52 ff. Cullmann, however, equates the 'naked' (II Cor. v. 3) state with the 'sleep' of I Thess. iv and I Cor. xv: there is no change in Paul's understanding of the parousia. Cf. also A. Schweitzer, *The Mysticism of Paul the Apostle* (London, 1931), p. 131; H. A. A. Kennedy, *St Paul's Conception of Last Things* (London, 1904), pp. 266–70.

II Cor. v has considerable bearing both upon the nature of Pauline anthropology and eschatology and upon the more specific question of the intermediate state. The commentators' exegetical differences arise for the most part in the presuppositions underlying the apostle's thought. Those (e.g. Dodd) who see a transition from Paul's earlier eschatology have a certain presumption to overcome. In view of Paul's parousia eschatology throughout his writings[1] 'ist es wahrscheinlich, daß er dennoch an einigen Stellen seiner Briefe, in welchen er doch auch immer an seiner Aeonen-Eschatologie festhält, plötzlich das Geschehen unmittelbar nach dem Tode in griechischem Sinne als definitiv entscheidend verkündigen würde?'[2]

I

In II Cor. iv. 10 f. the couplet,

> Always carrying the dying of Jesus in the body
> In order that the life of Jesus ἐν τῷ σώματι ἡμῶν φανερωθῇ.
> For we the living are ever given over to death for Jesus' sake
> In order that also the life of Jesus φανερωθῇ ἐν τῇ θνητῇ σαρκὶ ἡμῶν,

is followed by the assurance, which can be attested only by faith (13), that 'he who raised the Lord Jesus also ἡμᾶς σὺν Ἰησοῦ ἐγερεῖ and present us with you' (14).[3] Then occur (16–18) a series of antitheses:

> outer nature wasting... inner nature being daily renewed
> momentary affliction... eternal weight of glory (δόξης)
> transient 'seen' things... eternal 'unseen' things.

In Romans viii a similar pattern is observable. 'He who raised Christ Jesus from the dead will give life to your θνητὰ σώματα' (11). For the Spirit witnesses that, as fellow-heirs with Christ, we suffer with him that we may be glorified with him (συνδοξασθῶμεν) (17).[4] This consummation for which we groan (cf. II Cor. v. 4) is to be accomplished together with the renovation of the whole creation; while it is attested to us by the indwelling Spirit (cf. II Cor. v. 5), it belongs to the realm of the 'unseen',[5] not to the 'seen' (23–5; cf. II Cor. v. 7).

The basic divergency in the interpretation of II Cor. iv–v and Rom. viii relates to their eschatological perspective. Even Dodd admits, although reluctantly, a modified futurist reference in the latter passage.[6] The con-

---

[1] I Thess. iv–v; II Thess. ii; I Cor. xv; cf. II Cor. i. 9, 14; Eph. i. 21 f.; ii. 7; vi. 8; Phil. i. 6, 10; ii. 16; iii. 11, 20 f.; iv. 5; Col. iii. 4, 24; II Tim. iv. 8. The distinction which Robinson (*Jesus and His Coming*, p. 20) draws between the parousia and the 'day' seems to me to be, in the Pauline letters, an unwarranted dichotomy.

[2] J. N. Sevenster, 'Einige Bemerkungen über den "Zwischenzustand" bei Paulus', *New Test. Stud.* I (1954–5), 295. Cf. R. de Langhe, 'Judaïsme ou Hellénisme', *L'Attente du Messie* (Cerfaux et al.), Louvain, 1958, pp. 179–83.

[3] I.e. at His coming (Robinson, *Body*, p. 76).

[4] Cf. II Cor. i. 6; I Thess. iii. 3 f.; Phil. i. 29; II Tim. ii. 12.

[5] The 'unseen', i.e. the new aeon, present now as the 'hoped for', as ἀρραβών and ἐν Χριστῷ, will be 'manifest' only in the parousia (cf. Hebrews xi. 1, 39f.). Contrast ἀόρατος (Rom. i. 20; Col. i. 15f.); cf. *T.W.N.T.* v, 370. [6] C. H. Dodd, *Romans* (New York, 1932), p. 134.

currence of 'the redemption of our bodies' with the renovation of the cosmos identifies this passage completely with the Pauline aeon-eschatology which focuses God's redemptive action upon the parousia.[1] Whether II Cor. iv–v can be so understood depends upon the relationship one sees between Rom. viii and the above antitheses (and the further indicated parallels in II Cor. v). With the exception of the 'inner nature being daily renewed' (ἀνακαινοῦται) the right-hand column should be placed at the parousia if the parallel with Rom. viii is allowed.[2] The 'inner man' of II Cor. iv. 16 has been cited recently as an example of anthropological dualism in Paul.[3] This Greek interpretation, however, is quite un-Pauline and confuses ethics and psychology with metaphysics. As Robinson (*Body*, p. 76) has noted, 'this is exactly the same process of renewal that [Paul] alludes to in Romans xii. 1 f.': 'Present your *bodies* a living sacrifice....Be transformed by the renewing (ἀνακαινώσει) of your *minds*.' Mortal *soma*—the self viewed in its external physical relation to this age—is dying; the self in its relation to Christ is, even through and by its physical sufferings, being transformed. This transformation finds its ultimate goal at the parousia;[4] its process in this life, effected by the Spirit, is solely moral and psychological. It affects one's outlook on life and what the body *does*, not what the body *is*; this latter awaits the resurrection.[5]

Paul declares that—in the past—Christians were crucified with Christ, raised to life, translated into his kingdom, glorified, and made to sit with Christ in heaven.[6] The same experiences may be looked upon as future hope: 'That I may know him and the power of his resurrection, and may share his sufferings, becoming like him in his death, that if possible I may attain the resurrection from the dead' (Phil. iii. 10; cf. Rom. viii. 17 f.). Sometimes the perspective is mixed: 'If we have died with Christ, we believe that we shall also live with him' (Rom. vi. 8; cf. II Tim. ii. 11). The meaning of these different chronological perspectives, and their relationship, is the core question of the present eschatological debate.[7]

In its past reference the Christian's 'dying and rising' is coincident with

---

[1] Cf. N. Q. Hamilton, *The Holy Spirit and Eschatology in Paul* (Edinburgh, 1957), pp. 68 ff.; Cullmann, *Christ and Time*, pp. 102 ff.; I Thess. iv–v; I Cor. xv; cf. II Pet. iii. 10, 12 f.

[2] The use of φανερόω (II Cor. iv. 10) is not prejudicial to a parousia reference. 'When Christ shall appear (φανερωθῇ)...in his parousia...we shall be like him' (I John ii. 28; iii. 2) and 'will appear with him in glory' (Col. iii. 4). A 'crown of righteousness' will be given 'on that Day...to all who love his appearing (ἐπιφάνειαν) (II Tim. iv. 8; I Pet. v. 4). And 'in the appearing (ἐπιφανείᾳ) of his parousia' (II Thes. ii. 8) Christ will 'judge the living and the dead' (II Tim. iv. 1; cf. I Tim. vi. 14).

[3] S. Laeuchli, 'Monism and Dualism in the Pauline Anthropology', *Biblical Res.* III (1958), 19. He treats Rom. vii. 22, I Cor. xii. 1 ff., II Cor. iii. 18 in similar fashion.

[4] Rom. viii. 29; I Cor. xiii. 12 f.; cf. I John iii. 2.

[5] Although the Holy Spirit does, in temporal healing, retard on occasion the powers of death even here and now. Cf. O. Cullmann, *The Early Church* (London, 1956), pp. 165–73.

[6] Gal. ii. 20; Eph. ii. 5 f.; Col. i. 13; ii. 11 f.; Rom. viii. 30.

[7] For a recent discussion cf. W. G. Kümmel, 'Futurische und Präsentische Eschatologie im Ältesten Urchristentum', *New Test. Stud.* v (1958–9), 113–26.

conversion as it is manifest in baptism; it is always presented as a corporate event σὺν Χριστῷ and ἐν Χριστῷ.[1] Its present and future reference appears to involve the actualization of the corporate reality in the individual person. It is not without significance, therefore, that virtually every reference to the Christian's crucified and resurrected status is coupled with an ethical command. Colossians (ii. 20; iii. 1, 9 f., 12) provides a good example: 'If with Christ you died to the elemental spirits of the universe, why do you live as if you still belonged to the world?...If then you have been raised with Christ, seek the things that are above....Put to death the earthly....You have put off (ἀπεκδυσάμενοι) the old man and have put on (ἐνδυσάμενοι) the new man which is being renewed (ἀνακαινούμενον) in knowledge after the image of its creator....Put on (ἐνδύσασθε) then...compassion, kindness....'[2] Having been incorporated into the one organism, Christ's body, and destined to be conformed individually to Christ's image, the Christian is to 'grow up in every way into Him who is the Head' or controlling principle of the body.[3] Becoming 'one flesh' with Christ does not supersede or annul the 'individual' existence of the Christian.[4] This distinction between the Christian's individual and corporate existence provides the clue to understand Paul's— sometimes confusing—application of terms.

In his excellent treatise, *The Body*, Professor Robinson has rightly emphasized the 'corporate' existence of the Christian; one may question whether he has given due regard to the Christian's continuing individual existence and the significance this has for Paul's thought. It is agreed that 'nowhere in the New Testament has the resurrection of the body anything specifically to do with the moment of death. The key "moments" for this are baptism and the parousia.'[5] Robinson, however, goes on to speak of the resurrection of the body as a continuing process: 'Because of our incorporation into Christ the new solidarity is continually being built up within us. The condition of being "conformed" bodily (σύμμορφον) to the body of his glory (Phil. iii. 21; cf. Rom. viii. 29) is only the end of the process, begun at baptism, whereby Christ is being "formed" within us (μορφωθῇ, Gal. iv. 19).'[6] Now, it is by no means certain that Gal. iv. 19 refers to a present process (rather than to a parousia consummation)[7] and still less so that the renewal process in the Christian life should be spoken of as 'resurrection', a term which speaks to man in his mortality. The same verse (II Cor. iv. 16 f., 'being renewed'), which Robinson here cites in support of his view, he earlier (p. 76) interprets as 'exactly the same process of renewal' as Rom. xii. 1.

---

[1] E.g. Rom. vi; cf. II Cor. v. 17; Gal. iv. 26; Col. ii. 11 f.; Phil. iii. 20. Gal. ii. 20 perhaps is best translated 'I am con-crucified-with Christ' (Robinson, *Body*, p. 63).

[2] Cf. Rom. vi. 8, 11; viii. 9, 13, 29; I Cor. vi. 14, 18; xv. 49, 53 f.; II Cor. iii. 18; iv. 4; v. 2–4, 14 f.; Eph. ii. 5 ff.; iv. 1, 22 ff.

[3] Eph. iv. 15; cf. I Cor. xii. 27; Eph. i. 23; Rom. viii. 29.

[4] Cf. the husband–bride analogy in I Cor. vii. 14 ff.; II Cor. xi. 2, Eph. v. 22 ff.

[5] Robinson, *Body*, p. 79.   [6] Robinson, *Body*, pp. 80 f.

[7] The figure is that of an embryo coming to birth. Cf. Rom. viii. 29; Col. i. 18; I Cor. xv. 22 f.

There, as also in II Cor. iii. 18,[1] μεταμορφόω must be understood not as a physical–metaphysical change but as a moral and *weltanschaulich* (or psychological) transformation which the indwelling Spirit, the power of the new aeon, is effecting in the lives and minds of Christians.[2] Resurrection is always used, in this framework, with reference to a point action at conversion or parousia; never does Paul speak of it as a process which is now going on.

It is a mistake, therefore, to regard 'the inner nature being renewed' in II Cor. iv. 16 f. as implying an anthropological dualism (as Laeuchli)[3] or a progressive corporate resurrection (as Robinson). The verse is, as the parallel texts suggest, a contrast between the Christian, i.e. the total self, as he is still related (in his mortality) to the old aeon and the Christian as he is now also related (in his ethic and *Weltanschauung*) to the new aeon through the indwelling Spirit.[4] This distinction between resurrection, as point action, and moral–psychological renewal, as process, may appear to be mere semantic quibbling; but it has considerable importance for understanding Paul's eschatological thought world.

Paul pictures the corporate ἐν Χριστῷ reality as undergoing in the present time a twofold process of actualization in the individual Christian. As noted above, there is a progressive moral conformity to the character of Christ and, indeed, the very genuineness of one's status is determined by what he has done 'in the body';[5] similarly, the reality of the new aeon is being individually actualized in a psychological or *weltanschaulich* transformation in which the Christian mystery is increasingly apprehended and increasingly determinative for one's world and life view.

But, secondly, the old aeon also is being worked out in the Christian. Paul does not, strangely enough, view this as the remains of a corporeity ἐν 'Αδάμ but apparently regards it also as an aspect of the ἐν Χριστῷ existence. For, while the individual actualization of Christ's resurrection awaits the parousia, the present physical afflictions of the members of Christ's Body are an actualization of the suffering of the Head. It is not merely that we suffer

---

[1] It may be that 'die Brücke zwischen Gegenwart und Eschatologie steckt in ἀπὸ δόξης εἰς δόξαν', the latter referring to the consummation, *T.W.N.T.* ii, 254; cf. Rom. viii. 18, 29; I Cor. xv. 43, 49, Phil. iii. 21. The other meaning is indicated in Mark ix. 2.

[2] Cf. *T.W.N.T.* ii, 254 f.; iv, 766.   [3] *Op. cit.* p. 19.

[4] It is not difficult to grasp Paul's distinction between the self in its mortality (ἔξω ἄνθρωπος, II Cor. iv. 16) and the self in its ethico-intellectual perversion (παλαιὸς ἄνθρωπος, Rom. vi. 6; Eph. iv. 22; Col. iii. 9). Both refer to man as he is determined by the old aeon. With the latter is contrasted 'the new (καινός) man created in righteousness' and the new (νέος) man 'being renewed (ἀνακαινούμενον) in knowledge' (Eph. iv. 22; ii. 15; Col. iii. 10). The inner (ἔσω) man also is man in his ethical renewal and man in his ability to comprehend and know 'the love of Christ' (Rom. vii. 22; Eph. iii. 16 ff.); and in II Cor. iv. 16 the inner man is contrasted with the outer (ἔξω) man. Nevertheless while 'outer' and 'old' are obviously not to be equated, both 'new man' and 'inner man' refer to the self in its new aeon status and, as a process, to the self in its moral transformation and in its increasing apprehension and comprehension of the mystery of Christ. This pattern does not lend itself in the least to an anthropological dualism.

[5] II Cor. v. 10; cf. Rom. ii. 6 ff.; I Cor. ii. 13 ff.; Gal. v. 21; Eph. v. 5; Col. iii. 24.

'for Christ's sake' (διὰ 'Ιησοῦν, II Cor. iv. 11),[1] but that we 'share his suffering' (Phil. iii. 10) for the 'sufferings of Christ abound to us' (II Cor. i. 5).[2]

To participate in the body is also to participate in the blood (I Cor. x. 16), i.e. in the sacrificial death of Christ. To 'fill out' Christ is to 'fill up' his 'afflictions' (Col. i. 24). Indeed in the most obvious sense it is only in 'the likeness of his death' that we are at present united with him: 'the likeness of his resurrection' lies in the future (Rom. vi. 5).[3]

Present suffering yielding future resurrection glory is a fairly common idea and is the proper interpretation of II Cor. iv. 17.[4] Both realities can be understood in a literal—i.e. 'the most obvious'—sense. However, as present partakers of the about-to-be-revealed glory (Rom. viii. 18; I Pet. v. 1) we are already glorified,[5] comforted,[6] possessors of all things only[7] ἐν Χριστῷ. This corporate reality is vouchsafed to us individually by the Spirit (who is the ἀρραβών and ἀπαρχή of the coming new-age existence), but, until the parousia, is realized personally only in the exalted Lord, 'the ἀπαρχή of those who have fallen asleep', the 'first-born among many brethren'.[8]

The Christian's suffering then, and even his death, is no longer to be understood in terms of ἐν 'Αδάμ but rather of being 'crucified with Christ'. With this in mind Paul can speak of his own death as a sacrifice (Phil. ii. 17; II Tim. iv. 6) and of deceased brethren as having fallen asleep διὰ τοῦ 'Ιησοῦ.[9]

II

The exegesis of II Cor. v. 1–10 has been determined by the interpretation of two or three terms, namely, the 'house in the heavenlies' (1), the stripped or naked state (3 f.), and 'absence from the body' (8). Of these, the first probably has been most influential in the popular understanding of the passage.

By and large, commentators identify the 'house' with 'spiritual bodies' of individual Christians. Probably most would not speak of them as 'apparently waiting in store for us on the heavenly shelves'.[10] But, whether to be 'put on'

---

[1] Cf. II Thess. i. 5; Phil. i. 29; I Thess. iii. 3.

[2] Cf. Rom. xii. 1; Heb. xiii. 12 f.; I Pet. ii. 21; iv. 1, 13.

[3] Robinson, *Body*, p. 74.

[4] Cf. Rom. viii. 17 f.; II Thess. i. 5, 7; II Tim. ii. 12; Heb. xiii. 13 f.; I Pet. iv. 13.

[5] Rom. viii. 30; I Cor. xii. 26; cf. Eph. iii. 13; II Cor. iii. 18.

[6] II Cor. i. 5–7; cf. I Thess. iii. 6 f.

[7] II Cor. vi. 8–10.

[8] I Cor. xv. 20 ff.; Rom. viii. 29; cf. Hebr. ii. 8 ff.

[9] I Thess. iv. 14. Note the corresponding σὺν αὐτῷ. Cf. Rom. v. 11, 17; xv. 30; II Cor. i. 5; iv. 5 (WH mg.); v. 10; I Pet. ii. 5 where διά appears to involve, not merely agency, but a sphere of corporate relationship. 'To us the idea of being "with" Christ conveys something more external than that of being "in" him. But almost certainly it did not to Paul' (Robinson, *Body*, p. 62). In Phil. i. 23 de Langhe (*op. cit.* p. 182) compares 'with Christ' to the Old Testament expressions 'gathered to his people' (e.g. Gen. xxv. 7, 17) and 'slept with his fathers' (e.g. Deuteronomy xxxi. 16). On the relation of μετά and σύν cf. Dupont, *op. cit.* pp. 17 ff. 99.

[10] Lowe, *op. cit.* p. 136.

at death[1] or at the parousia,[2] οἰκία is understood to be the external shell of the soul or real self.[3] Certainly 'house' is used in this sense in the first-century Greek world,[4] and Paul might well employ the term 'tent-house' (οἰκία τοῦ σκήνους) to emphasize the transitory character of the present body.[5]

It may be questioned, however, whether the usage here has been understood when οἰκία is interpreted merely of the individual body. Moreover, serious objections arise if the corresponding 'house from heaven' is thought of in individual fashion. This house is described as a present possession (ἔχομεν),[6] a building from God (οἰκοδομήν), not made with hands (ἀχειροποίητος), eternal, and in the heavenlies. There are a number of considerations which compel the conclusion that Paul's primary thought is not of individual bodies at all, but of corporate solidarities which inhere in Adam and in Christ, the old aeon and the new aeon. First, 'whenever Paul uses the word οἰκοδομή (except in the purely figurative sense of "edification"), it means the Body of Christ, the Church (I Cor. iii. 9; Eph. ii. 21; iv. 12, 16), not an individual body'.[7] Second, οἴδαμεν (1) suggests that the teaching introduced is not novel—probably not even uniquely Pauline—but a well-known Christian concept to which he calls attention. Third, one finds such a concept in the complex of images expressed in the terms Body of Christ, the New Man, the New Temple; and these images are manifestly present in II Cor. v.

'Do ye not know (οἴδατε)', Paul asks earlier, 'that ye are God's temple?' (I Cor. iii. 16). This motif is taken up again in II Cor. vi. 16 ff. and is there supported by a *catena* of Old Testament *testimonia*.[8] The concept is deeply rooted not only in Pauline thought but in the substructure of New Testament thought-patterns generally, and probably finds its origin in the sayings of Jesus himself. It may not be without significance that three key words of II Cor. v. 1 are contained in Mark xiv. 58: 'We heard him say, "I will destroy (καταλύσω) this temple that is made with hands, and in three days I will build (οἰκοδομήσω) another, not made with hands (ἀχειροποίητον)".' 'Not made with hands' is a quasi-technical term in the New Testament pointing to the corporate realities of the new aeon. Used with 'house' or

[1] E.g. E. G. Selwyn, *The First Epistle of St Peter* (London, 1946), p. 190; Davies, *op. cit.* p. 318; Hettlinger, *op. cit.* pp. 193 f.; C. Masson, 'Immortalité de l'âme ou resurrection des morts?', *Revue de Théologie et de Philosophie*, VIII (1958), 250–67.

[2] E.g. Goudge, *op. cit.* p. 47; Lietzmann, *op. cit.* pp. 118 f.; R. Bultmann, *Exegetische Probleme des zweiten Korintherbriefes* (Uppsala, 1947), p. 12; F. V. Filson, 'Second Corinthians', *The Interpreters' Bible* (Nashville, 1953), X, 327.

[3] Cf. R. Bultmann, *Theology of the New Testament* (London, 1952), I, 202 f.

[4] E.g. Philo, *de praem.* 120; *de som.* I, 122; cf. Wisd. ix. 15; Bultmann, *Probleme*, p. 6.

[5] *T.W.N.T.* v, 135; cf. Job iv. 19.

[6] 'The fatal objection to taking verse 1 as speaking of the individual resurrection body is the present ἔχομεν', Robinson, *Body*, p. 77. See also A. Feuillet, 'La demeure céleste et la destinée des chrétiens (II Cor. v. 1–10)', *Recherches de Science Religieuse*, XLIV (1956), 161–92, 360–402.

[7] Robinson, *Body*, p. 76; cf. I Tim. i. 4 mg.

[8] Cf. E. E. Ellis, *Paul's Use of the Old Testament* (Edinburgh, 1957), pp. 90 ff., 108; Eph. ii. 19 ff.; v. 31 f.; I Pet. ii. 5 ff.

'temple', it refers to the corporate Body of Christ.[1] Stephen's polemic against the temple cultus centres in the assertion that God does not live in houses made with hands (Acts vii. 48 f.). God is building anew David's tent (ἀνοικοδομήσω τὴν σκηνήν, Acts xv. 16), which is the true tent, not made with hands (Heb. viii. 2).[2] In view of the use of σκηνή elsewhere in New Temple typology, it is not unreasonable to suppose that σκῆνος in II Cor. v. 1 has similar connotations. Also, the use of οἶκος (and its cognates) elsewhere in the New Testament in a corporate sense further substantiates this interpretation of the present context.[3]

It is most probable then that in II Cor. v. 1 ff. Paul has in mind the concept of the New Temple which views the Messianic Community in terms of the 'house of God'. In an interchange of the two images, New Temple and Body of Christ, the house from heaven (οἰκητήριον, II Cor. v. 2) or building of God (κατοικητήριον, Eph. ii. 22) here refers to those ἐν Χριστῷ as they are incorporated into the Body of Christ in whom the new aeon has been fully actualized and who alone is individually present in the heavenlies.[4] The corollary also follows: The 'tent-house' (II Cor. v. 1) envisions primarily not the individual self (although this is included) but the whole ἐν 'Αδάμ corporeity which stands under death.[5]

Paul's use of ἐνδύω supplements the pattern noted above. Christians 'put on' Jesus Christ when, at conversion, they were incorporated into him (Gal. iii. 27; cf. Col. iii. 10) and are commanded to actualize this in a continuing ethico-psychological transformation (Rom. xiii. 14);[6] the new aeon is to be metaphysically actualized when, at the parousia, death is swallowed up (κατεπόθη) and all ἐν Χριστῷ shall 'put on' immortality (I Cor. xv. 22 f., 53 f.). Paul's desire in II Cor. v. 2 ff. to 'put on' (ἐπενδύσασθαι) the heavenly house in order that mortality (θνητόν) may be swallowed up (καταποθῇ) by life is precisely parallel to I Cor. xv and should be understood of the parousia. While the 'tent-house' (as σῶμα ψυχικόν) and the 'house from heaven' (as σῶμα πνευματικόν) may be viewed in an individual perspective, this must be understood within the larger framework of the ἐν 'Αδάμ and ἐν Χριστῷ corporeity. This concept cannot be understood in terms of a gnostic or other anthropological dualism; for Paul posits neither a division of the self nor an escape from materiality at death but a 'changed' (ἀλλαγησόμεθα, I Cor.

---

[1] Cf. John ii. 19; Acts xvii. 24. Also, 'New Covenant' circumcision, not made with hands, is the death of Christ into which Christians have been incorporated. Cf. Col. ii. 11; Eph. ii. 11; Robinson, *Body*, p. 41.

[2] Heb. viii. 2 is translated 'servant of the saints' by some Church fathers; this may be more accurate than is now realized, namely servant of the saints, i.e. of the 'tent'. Cf. Heb. iii. 6; *contra*, O. Michel, *Der Brief an die Hebräer* (Göttingen, 1955), p. 185.

[3] Cf. *T.W.N.T.* IV, 887 f.; v, 149; Acts vii. 47 f.; I Tim. iii. 15; Heb. iii. 2 ff., 6.

[4] Cf. Feuillet, *op. cit.*; Eph. ii. 21; iii. 6.

[5] Cf. Matt. xxvi. 61; Mark xiv. 58. Bultmann (*Probleme*, pp. 10 f.) notes that καταλυθῇ may refer to the final destruction of the old aeon at the parousia. Cf. Matt. xxvi. 61; Mark xiv. 58; Phil. iii. 19 (ἐπίγεια).

[6] Cf. I Thess. v. 8; Eph. iv. 24; vi. 11; Col. iii. 12.

xv. 52)[1] psychosomatic organism which envelops and pervades the whole personality and finds its fulfilment in the deliverance of the whole man at the resurrection.[2]

III

Another concept fundamental for an understanding of the apostle's train of thought is that contained in the two words, γυμνός and ἐκδύω. γυμνός has usually been interpreted, in terms of an anthropological dualism, as the 'naked' or disembodied intermediate state;[3] in like fashion ἐκδύσασθαι cannot 'mean anything else than the parting with the body of flesh'.[4] While some commentators more accurately (as we hope to show) have identified γυμνός with the fate of unbelievers, the exegesis has been bound up with a body–soul dualism. We have here, writes Oepke, 'das Schicksal der Nichtgläubigen zu verstehen, die im Sterben, vor oder bei der Parousie, ihren irdischen Leib verlieren, ohne doch den Himmelsleib zu haben, welcher den Gläubigen bei der Parousie wartet'.[5] Although Paul (it is thought) derived the expression, and the dualism, from the Greek world,[6] he has modified it in the light of his Hebrew background: for Plato and Philo the 'nakedness' of disembodiment was the goal of life; for Paul it was patently undesirable, and his use of the term actually was a polemic against Gnostics in Corinth who depreciated material existence.[7]

The objection to this whole approach is that it presupposes an anthropological dualism absent from Paul elsewhere and that it is, in the present context, an awkward solution at best. What Paul shrinks from in v. 3 ('nakedness') he is said to embrace in v. 8 ('absence from the body').[8] This writer is convinced that the 'Greek trail' has been a false detour; the more

---

[1] Nor is the qualification, 'as a garment', in Heb. i. 12 (if original) to be taken to suggest a Greek dualism. It is a familiar Old Testament word picture: Ps. cii. 26; Isa. l. 9; li. 6. Cf. Michel, *Hebräer*, p. 58; Bultmann, *Probleme*, pp. 6, 10.

[2] Hettlinger (*op. cit.* p. 187) poses the *non sequitur* that Paul, by abandoning 'the identity of material elements' in I Cor. xv, undermines the logic of a 'material' resurrection altogether. Identity of atoms and materiality are surely not to be equated, and the whole chapter presupposes some kind of identity between the body sown and the body raised. Cf. I Cor. vi. 19 where this identity is basic to the argument. Also, it misrepresents Paul to interpret 'flesh and blood' (I Cor. xv. 50) as materiality. Cf. J. Jeremias, 'Flesh and Blood cannot inherit the Kingdom of God (I Cor. xv. 50)', in *New Test. Stud.* II, 151 ff.; Robinson, *Body*, pp. 20 f., 31 f., 78; Bultmann, *Theology*, I, 233 f.; Methodius, *Discourse on the Resurrection*, III, ii, 5 f. (Roberts and Donaldson, *Ante-Nicene Fathers*, Grand Rapids, 1951, VI, 374).

[3] E.g. Plummer, *op. cit.* pp. 147 ff.; Schweitzer, *Mysticism*, p. 134; J. Hering, *La Seconde Épître de Saint Paul aux Corinthiens* (Paris, 1958), p. 48; H. Lietzmann, *An die Korinther*, I–II (Tübingen, 1931), 120; cf. J. N. Sevenster, 'Some Remarks on the ΓΥΜΝΟΣ in II Cor. v. 3', *Studia Paulina* (J. de Zwaan *Festschrift*), Haarlem, 1953, p. 211.

[4] Kennedy, *op. cit.* p. 266. This, as far as the present writer is aware, is the unanimous conclusion of the commentators.

[5] *T.W.N.T.* II, 319; Cf. I, 744. So R. H. Charles, *Revelation*, I, 98: 'The soul of the faithless will appear naked in the next world.' Cf. W. Beyschlag, *N.T. Theology* (Edinburgh, 1896), II, 270.

[6] E.g. Plato, *Cratylus* 403 B; *Gorgias* 523 E, 524 D; Philo, *leg. alleg.* II, 55 ff.; Origen, *c. Celsum*, II, 43.

[7] Bultmann, *Probleme*, pp. 11 f.; *Theology*, I, 202.

[8] The attempts of Bultmann (*ibid.*), Hettlinger, *op. cit.* pp. 185, 191, Sevenster ('On ΓΥΜΝΟΣ', p. 207), and others to ease this contradiction have not been particularly convincing.

direct (and surely the more natural) route of New Testament and Septuagint usage provides a more fruitful approach.

It is not in Greek anthropology, but in Hebrew eschatology that the meaning of γυμνός and ἐκδύω in II Cor. v is to be found. In the Old Testament defeat and captivity were viewed as the judgement of God upon sin. Nakedness, a term used of the abbreviated dress of slaves and war captives, came to have this connotation of guilt and judgement.[1] Such attire might be adopted in symbolic proclamation of the coming calamity. Thus Isa. (xx. 2–4) goes 'naked' as a portent of God's verdict of destruction upon Egypt and Ethiopia; Micah (i. 8) does the same regarding Judah. In the latter may be the additional thought of the prophet's participation in the guilt and judgement of his people.[2] Sometimes the ethical symbolism emphasizes the sin-guiltiness of man in the presence of a holy God with the element of impending judgement less explicit or absent. Fallen Adam 'heard the sound' of God and hid because he was 'naked' (Gen. iii. 10); Israel, 'naked' of virtue, is clothed with God's covenant blessings (Ezek. xvi. 7 f.);[3] even Sheol is bared under God's discerning eye (Job xxvi. 6).

It is noteworthy that in the above passages γυμνός ('naked') is sometimes joined with ἐκδύω ('strip'),[4] sometimes with αἰσχύνη ('shame').[5] The last two are also found in combination. A singular instance occurs in Ezekiel where all three words are used in describing God's judgement on Jerusalem:

...that they may see all your nakedness (αἰσχύνην)...I will give you into the hands of your lovers and...they shall strip you (ἐκδύσουσιν)...and leave you naked and bare (γυμνὴν καὶ ἀσχημονοῦσαν) (Ezek. xvi. 37, 39).
And they shall also strip you (ἐκδύσουσιν)...and leave you naked and bare (γυμνὴ καὶ αἰσχύνουσα) (Ezek. xxiii. 26, 29).[6]

In the Old Testament, then, nakedness (or being stripped) and shame often denote the guilty under the glaring light of God's judgement and, used thus, are virtually equivalent terms. In late Judaism[7] and in the New Testament this equation continues, and the focus shifts from temporal to eschatological judgements which the former, in the old aeon, typified.[8] Thus, to be prepared

---

[1] E.g. Isa. xlvii. 3; Ezek. xvi. 37; xxiii. 29; Dan. iv. 30b LXX; Hos. ii. 3; Amos ii. 16; cf. Isa. iii. 17; Habakkuk iii. 13; Zephaniah ii. 14.   [2] Cf. also II Sam. xv. 30; xvi. 11 f.

[3] The ethical element is to be inferred (cf. Ezek. xvi. 36 f.) although physical redemption from captivity may be the central thought.   [4] Hos. ii. 3; Isa. xxxii. 11.

[5] Isa. xx. 4 f.; cf. Gen. ii. 25; Micah i. 11; Isa. xlvii. 3. Its synonym ἀσχημοσύνη is sometimes substituted in LXX-A (e.g. Ezek. xxiii. 18; Nahum iii. 5).

[6] Of further significance is the fact that cognates of ערה ('make naked') are often translated αἰσχύνη by the LXX. Cf. Isa. xliii. 3; Ezek. xvi. 36 f., 39; xxii. 10; xxiii. 10, 18, 29; Nahum iii. 5. ערם is always translated by γυμνός.

[7] This interpretation of some of the passages cited is present in the rabbis; e.g. Shab. 114a on Isa. xx. 2; Ex. R. 46, 4 on Ezek. xxiii. 26; Hos. ii. 5; Lam. R. 24, 2 on Isa. xxii. 8; xxxii. 11.

[8] At least one of these passages (Hos. ii. 3) is within a *testimonia* 'text plot' in frequent use by the early Christian community and interpreted there, in a passage parallel to II Cor. v. 1–10 (i.e. I Cor. xv. 55; Hos. xiii. 14), of the eschatological 'day of the Lord'. We may assume that other prophetic judgements of the old aeon were similarly understood (e.g. Joel ii. 26 f., 32; Acts ii. 19 ff.; Rom. x. 11 ff.).

for the Messianic banquet is to have a 'wedding garment' (Matt. xxii. 11). Without this white garb of righteousness even those within the professing community are naked and when Christ, as a thief, comes suddenly in his parousia, their nakedness and shame will be manifest (φανερωθῆ ἡ αἰσχύνη τῆς γυμνότητός σου).[1]

The ethical significance of γυμνός was properly understood in an earlier day.[2] But with the rising emphasis upon *Religionsgeschichte* the Platonic and Gnostic parallels came to dominate the exegesis. This later interpretation fits neither the immediate grammar[3] nor the eschatological theme of the passage. With the equation of 'nakedness' and 'shame' in mind a not unlikely commentary on II Cor. v. 3 may be found in the following paraphrased verses:

No one who believes in him will be stripped naked (καταισχυνθήσεται, Rom. x. 11).[4]

Abide in him, so that when he appears we may have confidence and not shrink from him in nakedness (αἰσχυνθῶμεν ἀπ᾽ αὐτοῦ) at his parousia (I John ii. 28).

Both γυμνός and ἐκδύω in II Cor. v have the judgement scene in view.[5] The opposite of being clothed upon by the house from heaven, i.e. the righteous Body of Christ, is not to be disembodied but to stand in the judgement ἐν ᾽Αδάμ, i.e. in the Body that is naked in guilt and shame. It is not at death but at the parousia that those without the wedding garment (Matt. xxii. 11), the spiritual body (I Cor. xv. 44, 53 f.), the heavenly house (II Cor. v. 1 f.) to put on will be discovered stripped and naked (II Cor. v. 3 f.).[6]

---

[1] Rev. iii. 17 f.; cf. xvi. 15; Micah i. 11; Heb. iv. 13.

[2] J. Calvin, *The Corinthians* (Grand Rapids, 1948), II, 218; H. Ewald, *Die Sendschreiben des Apostels Paulus* (Göttingen, 1857), p. 271; H. Cremer, *Biblio-Theological Lexicon* (Edinburgh, 1880), p. 168; cf. A. Jülicher *Festschrift* (1927), pp. 93 ff.; *T.W.N.T.* I, 744. Also cf. GT xx. 37!

[3] Cremer (*op. cit.*) points out that οὐ γυμνοί is co-ordinate with ἐνδυσάμενοι (not ἐνδεδυμένοι), i.e. to be found 'clothed' means to be found 'not naked', and, therefore, 'if we are not found naked' is the condition prerequisite to ἐπενδύσασθαι of *v.* 2. γυμνοί, then, must be taken in an ethical—not metaphysical—sense. Also, 'we do not want to be stripped' cannot properly be softened to 'not that we would...'; cf. Hettlinger, *op. cit.* p. 191.

[4] Cf. Rom. ix. 33. Isa. xxviii 16 refers to a deliverance from judgement, and the LXX (followed by the New Testament) translates חוּשׁ ('flee') by καταισχύνω, probably with the same sense as the above cited contexts. Cf. I Sam. xx. 38 f. and Ps. lv. 9 where חוּשׁ may, as a double meaning, signify 'flee'. So Brown–Driver–Briggs on Isa. xxviii. 16.

[5] I Cor. xv. 37 is no support for the common exegesis of II Cor. v. 3. 'Naked grain' is a completely different imagery and, in any case, refers not to a disembodied soul but to the present body. Nor does the Pauline compound, ἀπεκδύομαι, when used of death (namely putting off 'the body of flesh' or 'the old man', Col. ii. 11; iii. 9), imply a dualism. Both 'flesh' and 'the old man', as a number of studies have shown (e.g. W. G. Kümmel, *Das Bild des Menschen im Neuen Testament*, Zürich, 1948, pp. 22 f.; Robinson, *Body*, pp. 17–26, 31 f.; Bultmann, *Theology*, I, 232 ff.), refer to the whole man in his sinful and mortal relation to the old aeon and mean here simply our identification with Christ's death. Perhaps judgement (of the body of the flesh) is the thought of Col. ii. 11; certainly so in Col. ii. 15. Cf. E. K. Simpson and F. F. Bruce, *Ephesians and Colossians*. (Grand Rapids, 1957), pp. 235, 239 f.

[6] Cf. Robinson, *Body*, p. 77: 'Εὑρίσκεσθαι is almost a technical term for being "dis-covered" at the parousia.' Cf. I Pet. i. 7; II Pet. iii. 14; Phil. iii. 9.

IV

The assumption that 'away from the body' (ἐκδημέω, II Cor. v. 8) describes the intermediate state may be traced throughout the history of the exegesis[1] and is, as far as the present writer is aware, the consensus of all modern opinion. In view of the influence of Greek philosophy from a very early period one would expect the exegesis to take this direction. Not all, however, have been entirely comfortable in relating the verse to Paul's eschatological views elsewhere or to the present context.[2] Certainly Paul never views death as divorcing Christians from Christ,[3] but this can be so only because their incorporation into the heavenly body of Christ guarantees their resurrection. Although the corporate relation remains inviolate, in the individual death continues to reign. If the dead are not raised, those 'who have died in Christ have perished' (I Cor. xv. 18). Only at the parousia will the scripture be fulfilled, 'Death is swallowed up in victory' (I Cor. xv. 54). It becomes necessary, therefore, to scrutinize anew the traditional interpretation. If the foregoing exegesis of II Cor. v is correct, it opens the way to a different understanding of the present verse.

On a number of occasions Paul uses σῶμα to refer to the self in its solidarity with sin and death. There is usually a qualifying phrase such as the mortal body (Rom. vi. 12), the body of sin (Rom. vi. 6), of death (Rom. vii. 24), of humility (Phil. iii. 21), of dishonour (I Cor. xv. 43), or the natural body (I Cor. xv. 44f.). But this is not always the case; and even the immediate context speaks of deeds done 'in the body', i.e. in the mortal earthly life.[4] Robinson correctly interprets II Cor. v. 6: '"At home in the body" means "in the solidarities and securities of earthly existence".'[5]

It is probably a misconception to identify 'away from the body' (II Cor. v. 8) with the intermediate state at all. Rather, 'away' should be understood merely as absence from the solidarities of the mortal body, the σῶμα ψυχικόν; and as the earlier verses show, 'at home with the Lord' with which it is equated has reference to the σῶμα πνευματικόν life (I Cor. xv. 44) in which the solidarities of the new aeon are realized.[6] Thus, the desire of Paul in v. 8 is identical with that which he expressed in v. 4, namely to be 'clothed upon' at the parousia.[7] This interpretation is borne out in v. 7 where 'away from the Lord' and 'at home with the Lord' are contrasted as 'faith' and 'sight'[8] and, further, in vv. 9f. where 'at home' apparently refers to the parousia judgement.[9]

---

[1] It is found as early as Clement of Alexandria (*Stromata*, IV, xxvi) and Tertullian (*de resur. carnis*, XLIII).   [2] E.g. II Cor. v. 4 (*N.B.* ἐκδύω).

[3] Cf. de Langhe, *op. cit.* p. 182; Feuillet, *op. cit.* p. 395; Romans viii. 38; xiv. 8 f.; Phil. i. 23.

[4] II Cor. v. 10; cf. Robinson, *Body*, p. 29; Rom. viii. 13; Col. ii. 11; Heb. xiii. 3.

[5] *Ibid.*   [6] Cf. Sevenster, 'Zwischenzustand', p. 296 (cf. above, p. 212, n. 2); *T.W.N.T.* II, 63.

[7] Note also the repeated use of οἶδα in v. 1 and v. 6.

[8] The 'vision of God' is realized at the parousia. Cf. Rom. viii. 24; I Cor. xiii. 12; Heb. ii. 8 f. (I Cor. xv. 25 ff.); I Pet. i. 5, 8; I John iii. 2 f.

[9] Some commentators, logically impelled by their 'intermediate state' exegesis of the preceding verses, take II Cor. v. 10 to refer to a judgement at death—a brand new concept in Pauline thought.

V

The structure of II Cor. v. 1–10 forms a strikingly coherent series of antitheses which are continued from II Cor. iv, and which contrast the corporate existence of Christians ἐν 'Αδάμ and ἐν Χριστῷ. The individual actualization of the latter corporeity at the parousia is always in view.[1] On the one hand man in his tent-house (1) mortality (5) faces, in the final abolition of the old aeon, Adamic nakedness (3) and dissolution (1). His hope lies in his solidarity with the new aeon through the resurrected body of Christ. Yet for those in the mortal σῶμα (6) this remains hope, apprehended by faith (7), attested by good works (10), and actualized only in the ἀρραβών of the indwelling Spirit (5). Paul yearns for the day when mortality shall be swallowed up by life (4), faith shall become sight (7), 'away' shall become 'at home' (8), when the solidarities of the new aeon shall be individually actualized in putting on the σῶμα πνευματικόν, the house from heaven (2). This consummation shall come in the judgement (10) when the Day shall reveal every man's status (I Cor. iii. 13).

If one recognizes that, as in the concept of corporate solidarity generally,[2] a certain oscillation between the 'corporate' and the 'individual' is intertwined in Paul's thought-pattern, the antitheses of II Cor. v. 1–10 may be visualized in the following manner:

ἐν 'Αδάμ	ἐν Χριστῷ
the old aeon	the new aeon
tent-house	house from heaven
naked	clothed
mortality	life
faith	sight
at home in the body	away from the body
away from the Lord	at home with the Lord
in the body	at Christ's judgement seat

The idea of a 'spiritual' resurrection at death continues to be a widely accepted interpretation of Paul (even among those who give a technical place to a future bodily resurrection). This view, however, fails to appreciate the truth that Lüdemann and Kabisch saw almost a century ago: redemption

Others, recognizing the incongruity of this interpretation with Paul's eschatology, more properly apply it to the 'last day'. Cf. Kennedy, op. cit. p. 193; Lietzmann, op. cit. p. 122; Knox, op. cit. p. 141; Schweitzer, Mysticism, p. 310; Bultmann, Theology, I, 288; Cullmann, Christ and Time, p. 23; Robinson, Body, p. 19.

[1] Paul's concern that some Christians may be found 'naked' in the judgement is not contrary to his teaching on predestination or perseverance (Lietzmann, op. cit. p. 119). It is only the recognition, expressed elsewhere, that one's awareness of election is based upon subjective and existential criteria —genuine profession, witness of the Spirit, good works. One may deceive oneself. Cf. I Cor. ix. 27; II Cor. vi. 1; xiii. 5; Gal. iv. 11; Phil. iii. 12 f.; I Thess. iii. 5; II Tim. ii. 19; iv. 7. All in all, Paul is confident; II Cor. v. 5; cf. Phil. i. 6.

[2] Cf. the recent study of corporate solidarity in Pauline thought: R. P. Shedd, Man in Community (London, 1959), pp. 38 ff.

for Paul is physical.[1] While its advocates speak of Jerusalem, one suspects that the accent is Athenian.

Although the present passage has been a means to interpret Paul's 'developed' theology in this fashion, the parallels in Rom. viii and I Cor. xv alone are of such character as to cast grave doubt upon such exegesis. And if the above analysis is correct, II Cor. v cannot be used at all to illustrate a changed Pauline theology of the intermediate state: the passage simply does not deal with the intermediate state. The contrasts throughout are between this age and the age-to-come and are completely within the framework of Paul's parousia eschatology and his concept of corporate solidarity. Perhaps, as Professor Davies suggests,[2] the idea of an intermediate state has no place in Paul's thought here; but if so, it has an explanation very different from that which Davies has given. It must be understood, as Cullmann's valuable essay has suggested,[3] in terms of an altered or suspended time factor for the dead and not as an anticipated fulfilment at death of the parousia consummation. Paul's hope here, as throughout his epistles, is not in the abiding individual but in the abiding Christ; not in the immortal soul of Platonic idealism, but in 'the God who can bring the dead to life and can call to Himself the things that do not exist as though they did' (Rom. iv. 17, Williams).

[1] Cf. Schweitzer, *Interpreters*, p. 63.
[2] Davies, *op. cit.* p. 318.
[3] Cullmann, *Immortality*, p. 57.

CHAPTER THREE

THE AUTHORSHIP OF THE PASTORALS:
A RESUME AND ASSESSMENT OF RECENT TRENDS

I

Since the eighteenth century, the letters to Timothy, along with Titus, have been designated the "Pastoral" Epistles in recognition of their distinct character and content. Such is their similarity that, with minor exceptions, the consensus of opinion has been that in the question of genuineness the three epistles stand or fall together. Introduced with the familiar phrase, 'Paul an apostle of Christ Jesus,' they give a *prima facie* claim to be writen by the great apostle to the Gentiles. And from the second to the nineteenth century they were, without exception, so regarded. It is true that Marcion's abbreviated canon (*c.* A.D. 140) did omit them, most likely because they were private rather than church letters or (as his other omissions) because of doctrinal reasons. Also, one Pauline codex (P46) may have lacked them. But, on the whole, the witness of the patristic period is as strong as for the other Paulines with the exception of Rom. and I Cor. Modern criticism has rested its case almost altogether upon other grounds. If evidence external to the letters were the only criterion no serious question ever would have been lodged against them.

The genuineness of the Pastorals was first questioned by Schmidt (1805), Schleiermacher (1807), and Eichhorn (1812) for stylistic and linguistic reasons. The spread through Germany and Holland of this type of criticism, which sought to determine authenticity on philological grounds, resulted in the rejection of most of Paul's letters in the succeeding decades. Some scholars, discounting all of them, regarded even Paul himself as a figment of second-century imagination. The argument against the Pastorals was definitively stated in a German commentary by H. J. Holtzmann (1880), and this continues to be the standard frame of reference for the non-Pauline point of view. During this period most Anglo-American scholars, guided perhaps by Lightfoot's essay,[1] regarded the epistles as Pauline. Not until Harrison's critique (1921) of the language and style did the pendulum swing the other way. In the receding tide of radical criticism since the turn of the century only the Pastorals, the first to be questioned, are still held to be spurious by most students; and even here there are signs of a growing dissatisfaction with the methods and conclusions of the older criticism.

On the present scene four positions have commanded a significant following, including the assent and espousal of notable critical scholars. (1) Some continue to view the Pastorals as second-century writings with no Pauline con-

---

[1] J. B. Lightfoot, *Biblical Essays* (London, 1904), pp. 397-410.

tent except that which has filtered through the mind of an unknown disciple imitating his master.[2] (2) In more favour — and probably the most popular viewpoint — are those who consider a number of verses to be genuine Pauline fragments but conclude that the major content is from the hand of an early second-century Paulinist.[3] (3) Still closer to the traditional estimate are a number of writers who account for the stylistic differences in the Pastorals by positing Paul's use of an amanuensis or secretary; the content of the letters, however, is genuinely Pauline.[4] (4) Finally, a small group argue anew that any changes in style and content may be adequately accounted for within the framework of a direct dictation by the apostle.[5]

II

Objections to the Paulinity of the Pastorals have focused upon (1) the historical situation, (2) the type of false teaching condemned, (3) the stage of church organization, (4) the vocabulary and style, and (5) the theological viewpoint of the letters. The historical allusions are not numerous. In I Tim. (i. 3) Paul recently had made a trip from Ephesus to Macedonia. Titus (i. 5; iii. 12 f.) reveals that, having been in Crete, he was acquainted with the problems there; he was soon to be at Nicopolis, a city northwest of Corinth, where he desired Titus to meet him. Tychicus and Apollos, with whom Paul had been associated during the Ephesian ministry (Acts xix. 1 ff.; I Cor. xvi. 12; Acts xx. 4; cf. Eph. vi. 21; Col. iv. 7), are mentioned. While I Tim. and Titus have, on the face of it, a provenance of Achaia or Macedonia, II Tim. (i. 17) is written from prison, presumably in Rome, to the Aegean area from which Paul recently had come (cf. II Tim. iv. 11 f., 19).

Two factors in the historical situation weighed against the authenticity of the epistles in the minds of the earlier critics. (1) They despaired of fitting the experiences into the narrative of Acts and (2) some events appeared actually to be in conflict with or an imitation of the Lucan material. For example, Acts (xx. 1, 3 f.; cf. xix. 22) knows only two trips to Macedonia after the Ephesian ministry, and in neither is Timothy said to be left behind in Ephesus (I Tim. i. 3). There is no mention of a mission to Crete which Titus (i. 5) presupposes. Further, the attestation of a release from the imprisonment of Acts 28 is late and hazardous to use as a setting for the Pas-

---

2 E.g., H. J. Holtzmann, *Die Pastoralbriefe* (Leipzig, 1880); M. Dibelius, *Die Pastoralbriefe* (Tübingen, 1931), p. 6.

3 E.g., P. N. Harrison, *The Problem of the Pastoral Epistles* (London, 1921); B. S. Easton, *The Pastoral Epistles* (New York, 1947); E. F. Scott, *The Pastoral Epistles* (London, 1948), p. xxii.

4 E.g., O. Roller, *Das Formular der paulinischen Briefe* (Stuttgart, 1933); J. Jeremias, *Die Briefe an Timotheus und Titus* (Göttingen, 1947); P. Feine-J. Behm, *Einleitung in das Neue Testament* (Leipzig, 1950).

5 E.g., G. Thoernell, *Pastoralbrevens aekthet* (Goeteborg, 1931); F. Torm, *Die Psychologie der Pseudonymität im Hinblick auf die Literatur des Urchristentums* (Gütersloh, 1932); A. Schlatter, *Die Kirche der Griechen im Urteil des Paulus* (Stuttgart, 1936); *The Church in the New Testament Period* (London, 1955); W. Michaelis, *Einleitung in das Neue Testament* (Bern, 1946); cf. J. de Zwaan, *Inleiding tot het Nieuwe Testament* (Haarlem, 1948); S. Lyonnet, 'De arte litteras exarandi apud antiquos', *Verbum Domini* 34 (1956), 3-11; D. Guthrie, *The Pastoral Epistles* (Grand Rapids, 1957).

torals. Even if such a release is accepted, the epistles themselves appear to be a faulty imitation of Acts, citing the same cities and friends of the earlier mission.

In the positive criticism of the Tübingen School the heresies condemned in the Pastorals were identified with a second-century Gnosticism, and their true historical setting was thereby to be obtained. The church organization too was thought to reflect a type of monarchical episcopate which could not have developed in the apostolic age. The criticisms which have been most effective in recent years relate to the language and style of the letters and to their theological concepts. It is not merely the large number of words lacking elsewhere in Paul: even known words often are used with a different significance, structure, and frequency. For example, 'faith', which elsewhere in the Pauline corpus signifies 'trust', means in the Pastorals a body of doctrine (I Tim. iv. 1, 6; Titus i. 13). Good works are given a centrality unlike the writer of Galatians and Romans. Here we have, says Dibelius, a Christianity of orthodoxy and good works; and in similar vein James Denney writes, 'Saint Paul was inspired, but the writer of these epistles is sometimes only orthodox.'[6]

III

In recent years changing tides and countercurrents in New Testament critical studies have cast the 'Pastoral Problem' in a different light. The considered opinion of so notable a scholar as W. F. Albright that 'there is no longer any concrete evidence for dating a single New Testament book after the seventies or eighties of the first century'[7] flies in the face of much that has been asserted about these epistles. Bo Reicke's argument[8] that the organization of the early Church, like the Jewish groups from which it sprang, was a complex structure from the beginning undermines from a new quarter the view that the 'developed' ecclesiology of the Pastorals reflects a post-apostolic period. Harrison's 'word statistics,' long a pillar in the case against genuineness, have been subjected by Professor Metzger to sharp and telling criticisms.[9] Finally, in the light of the sketchiness of the Book of Acts[10] the *a priori* assumption that it can be used as a touchstone for Paul's life history falls considerably short of a 'first principle' for critical studies.

According to Acts, Paul spent between five and seven years in the Aegean area (*c.* A.D. 51-58), most of it in Ephesus and Corinth. Acts mentions only a trip to Jerusalem following the first sojourn in Corinth and the trip to Greece preceding his final visit and arrest in Jerusalem. But from the Corinthian and 'Captivity' letters other trips are to be inferred. The whole province of Asia

---

6 Dibelius, *op. cit.*, p. 3; J. Denney, *The Death of Christ* (London, 1902), pp. 202 f.

7 W. F. Albright, 'Return to Biblical Theology', *The Christian Century*, lxxv (1958), 1330.

8 Bo Reicke, 'The Constitution of the Primitive Church in the Light of Jewish Documents', *The Scrolls and the New Testament*, ed. K. Stendahl (New York, 1957), pp. 143-156.

9 B. M. Metzger, 'A Reconsideration of Certain Arguments against the Pauline Authorship of the Pastoral Epistles', *The Expository Times*, lxx (1958-59), 91-94.

10 Cf. G. S. Duncan, *St. Paul's Ephesian Ministry* (New York, 1930), pp. 95-107.

was evangelized (Acts xix. 10), and it is most natural to suppose that not only the work in the Lycus Valley but also missions (or embassies) to Crete and Nicopolis occurred during this period (cf. Titus i. 5; iii. 12).

It is more difficult to date the letters themselves during the Aegean ministry. One need not interpret Luke's phrase, 'day and night' (Acts xx. 31), in literalist fashion, but is there room for a winter at Nicopolis (Titus iii. 12)? And the detailed instructions of I Tim. indicate more than a temporary absence from Asia. The implication in II Tim. (iv. 13, 20) that Paul recently had been in the East does not fit the framework of Acts (xxi. 29; xxiv. 27; xxviii. 30). It is not impossible to place I Tim. and Titus in the period following Paul's final departure from Ephesus (Acts xx. 1) as Duncan tentatively suggests.[11] But the traditional post-Acts dating of all three letters is more probable, and most critical questions have been addressed to this view.

The abrupt close of Acts has been understood by some to indicate the release of Paul, by others his immediate martyrdom; either view seems more supported by the particular writer's mood than by any persuasive inference from the text. The tradition of a release, which is attested at least by A.D. 170-190[12] (I Clement v. 5-7 is uncertain), is not of the highest evidential value; but to discount it as imaginary reflection on Rom. xv. 24, as Harrison does,[13] is simply second guessing. If released, would Paul have journeyed east to the same Aegean cities, with the same associates, and in similar circumstances? Harrison answers, 'impossible repetition'; Guthrie replies, 'more surprising if otherwise.'[14] As the above discussion indicates, the historical situation presupposed by the letters poses some questions whose answers must remain problematical. The questions are not, in and of themselves, such as to raise serious doubt; and in the case against genuineness this argument bears at best only a supporting role.

The type of false teaching and the stage of church organization, in past years strong arguments against the Pastorals, have less weight today. Baur's identification of the heresy with second century Gnosticism is now generally recognized to be mistaken, and even Dibelius[15] concedes that this argument can no longer be used to show the spuriousness of the letters. Actually the error seems to reflect a gnosticizing Judaism (cf. I Tim. i. 7; Titus i. 10, 14 f.; iii. 9) not unlike that in Colossians (ii. 16 ff.). R. McL. Wilson's[16] recent study has shown that these tendencies were wide-spread in the Jewish *diaspora* of the first century; and according to Albright, 'Gnosticism had already developed some of its most pronounced sects well before the Fall of Jerusalem.'[17]

11 G. S. Duncan, 'Paul's Ministry in Asia — The Last Phase', *New Testament Studies*, 3 (1956-7), 211-218.

12 The Muratorian Canon; The Acts of Peter III.

13 Harrison, *op. cit.*, p. 108.

14 *Ibid.*, p. 111; Guthrie, *op. cit.*, p. 22.

15 Dibelius, *op. cit.*, p. 2.

16 R. McL. Wilson, *The Gnostic Problem* (London, 1958), pp. 74, 176.

17 W. F. Albright, 'Recent Discoveries in Palestine and the Gospel of John', *The Background of the New Testament and its Eschatology*, ed. W. D. Davies (Cambridge, 1956), p. 163.

If Zahn's[18] older (but relevant) appraisal is accepted, there is nothing re-
sembling this Jewish heresy in the post-apostolic period.

Heretical tendencies and movements were present from the beginning in
the Pauline churches. If one assumes the early date of Galatians, churches of
that area were infected with the Judaizing heresy within months of their
founding. Scarcely had the echoes of the apostle's voice died away when some
at Thessalonica went astray in a false teaching akin to that mentioned in
II Tim. ii. 18 (cf. II Thess. ii. 2). The heresy in Colossae made serious in-
roads within a very few years. Even when Paul was present in Ephesus some
professing Christians continued their 'magical arts,' and as he left, he feared
that the wolves were ready to pounce (Acts xix. 18 f.; xx. 29 f.). Considering
the type of heresy revealed in the Pastorals and the character of the apostolic
age, it is quite gratuitous to interpret this apostasy as a gradual departure of
long established churches.

The church organization of I Tim. (iii. 1 ff.) and Titus (i. 5 ff.) refers to the
offices of bishop, elder, and deacons; the first two terms appear to be used
interchangeably as they are in Acts (xx. 17, 28; cf. Titus i. 5, 7). There is also
an official 'service order' of widows. This function is not specifically mentioned elsewhere in the apostolic literature although it may possibly be in-
fered from such passages as Acts vi. 1; ix. 39, 41 (cf. Luke ii. 37). The reference to bishops and deacons in Phil. i. 1 (cf. I Thess. v. 12) corroborates the
evidence in Acts (xiv. 23; xx. 17, 28) that the officers of Pauline churches were
not unlike those mentioned in the Pastorals. Of course one can, as Easton
does,[19] simply excise as 'anachronisms' those portions of Acts which counter
his theory; but this procedure can hardly yield a satisfactory solution. Some
remain convinced that the singular 'bishop' (I Tim. iii. 2), the ban on
'neophytes' holding office (I Tim. iii. 6), and the local leaders' function as
tradition-bearers (II Tim. ii. 2; Titus i. 9) witness to a second-century monarchical episcopate. But in the light of I Tim. v. 17 the singular 'bishop' probably should be interpreted as a generic term,[20] and I Tim. iii. 6 would apply to
any church over a few years old. Nor does the idea of local leaders as tradition-bearers require a post-apostolic setting. Cullmann's essay, 'The Tradition,'[21] once more has pointed out that 'tradition' was not something which
succeeded 'charismatic gifts' in the Church; both were present in the earliest
period as coordinate functions. It would be quite fitting for the apostle at
the close of life to make such provisions as are indicated in the Pastorals. In
view of Professor Reicke's article mentioned above, it is no longer adequate
to view ecclesiastical organization of the early Church as an unilinear development from democracy to episcopate; there seems to be no strong 'ecclesiastical'
argument forbidding an early date to these letters. Michaelis[22] is convinced,
rather, that the omission of certain questions (e.g. baptismal practices, the

---

[18] T. Zahn, *Introduction to the New Testament* (Grand Rapids, 1953 [1909]), II, 115.
[19] Easton, *op. cit.*, p. 254.
[20] Cf. Michaelis, *op. cit.*, p. 254.
[21] O. Cullmann, *The Early Church* (London, 1956), pp. 59-99.
[22] Michaelis, *op. cit.*, pp. 254 f.

observance of the Lord's Supper) important for the Church in the post-apostolic times is an argument for a date consistent with genuineness.

In the rising cloud of doubt overshadowing earlier reconstructions, the arguments of 'language and style' and 'theological concepts' have continued to jut out in the minds of most students as clear and present obstacles to a verdict of genuineness. Harrison, whose *Problem of the Pastoral Epistles* has been most influential in Anglo-American scholarship, based his case against genuineness quite squarely upon language and style. (1) Of some 848 words in the three letters, 306 are not found elsewhere in the Pauline literature, (2) 175 in no other New Testament writing. (3) Many words and phrases characteristic of the apostle are missing (e.g. the righteousness of God, the body of Christ), and (4) the grammar and style of the letters varies considerably from the other Paulines. Moreover, (5) some sixty of the 175 Hapaxes (words found only in the Pastorals) occur in the second-century Fathers.

Although Harrison's arguments were for the most part favourably received in the English speaking world, they found a different reception on the Continent. Dibelius,[23] no friend to Pauline authorship, questioned the adequacy of the statistical method as an argument against authenticity. Michaelis,[24] in a well-reasoned critique, argued that Harrison produced the results he did simply because his faulty and arbitrary methodology demanded those results. For example, Harrison found an excessively high number of 'Hapaxes per page' in the Pastorals; but he neglected to mention that these letters have a high total number of 'words per page'; and that in proportion to 'words per book' the percentage of Hapaxes in the Pastorals was not greatly different from other Pauline letters. In Britain, Montgomery Hitchcock[25] made the rather embarrassing discovery that the vocabulary of second-century writings shows a closer relationship to I Corinthians (and to Colossians and Ephesians for that matter) than to the Pastorals. Most recently Donald Guthrie, in a 'penetrating critique of Harrison's linguistic argument'[26] sums up the latter's grammatical and stylistic conclusions : 'The same arguments could equally well prove the non-Pauline character of undisputed Pauline epistles, and secondly . . . these statistics take no account of mood and purpose.'[27] Professor Bruce Metzger[28] has called attention to a volume by a professional statistician which, if its results are accepted, has serious consequences for Harrison's whole hypothesis. The Cambridge professor,[29] after careful investigation into the use of vocabulary-style comparisons to determine authorship, concludes that to obtain reliable data the treatise under

23 Dibelius, *op. cit.*, p. 2.

24 W. Michaelis, 'Pastoralbriefe und Wortstatistik', *Zeitschrift für die neutestamentliche Wissenschaft*, 28 (1929), 69 ff.

25 F. R. M. Hitchcock, 'Tests for the Pastorals', *Journal of Theological Studies*, xxx (1928-29), 279.

26 Metzger, *op. cit.*, p. 94. However, cf. *NTS* 6 (1959-60), 1-15.

27 Guthrie, *op. cit.*, p. 227.

28 Metzger, *op. cit.*, p. 93.

29 G. U. Yule, *The Statistical Study of Literary Vocabulary* (Cambridge, 1944).

study must be at least 10,000 words long. The Pastorals fall far short of this minimum.

Some 25 years ago Otto Roller investigated the nature and practice of letter writing in the Roman world and gave birth to a new hypothesis. He found that an author often employed an amanuensis who was given a variable degree of freedom in composing the final document from dictated notes. The author then corrected it and added a closing greeting (cf. Gal. vi. 16). If Paul employed a trusted amanuensis in writing the Pastorals (the affinity with the language of Luke has long been noted), this 'secretary hypothesis' may be the answer to the stylistic peculiarities found there. It has proved persuasive to some writers (e.g., Jeremias, Behm) although others (e.g., Michaelis) contend that Paul's unique style elsewhere indicates a direct dictation and that the style of the Pastorals may be fully accounted for within this framework. In any case, this hypothesis is free from some of the disabilities of the 'fragment theory', and it seeks to found itself in known literary habits of the first-century world.

The major theological concepts of the letters are recognized by all to be 'Pauline', and those rejecting their genuineness posit a devoted disciple as the author. The writer 'declares that Christ gave himself for our redemption, that we are justified not by our own righteousness but by faith in Christ, that God called us by his grace before the world was, and that we are destined to an eternal life on which we can enter even now. These are no mere perfunctory echoes of Pauline thought' (cf. I Tim. vi. 11 ff.; iii. 16; II Tim. i. 8 ff.; ii. 11 ff.; Titus ii. 11 ff.; iii. 5) .[30] The personal references also appear to be of Pauline coinage (cf. I Tim. i. 12 ff.; ii. 7; II Tim. i. 3 ff.; ii. 8 ff.; iv. 6 ff., 17 f.) , as are the teaching on baptism (Titus iii. 5-7; cf. Eph. v. 26) and the state (Titus iii. 1; I Tim. ii. 1 ff.; cf. Rom. xiii. 1 ff.) . The absence of the 'body' concept (in its theological significance also lacking in Galatians, I and II Thessalonians) is thought by Robinson[31] to be decisive against Pauline authorship; but the presence of the intimately related 'Temple typology' would seem to weaken any argument of this sort (I Tim. i. 4 mg.; iii. 15; v. 4; II Tim. ii 19; cf. John ii. 20 f.; I Cor. iii. 16 f.; II Cor. vi. 16; Eph. ii. 19 ff) .

Different concepts occur mainly in the use of terms not found in Paul and the absence of others characteristic of the apostle: For example, God pictured as Saviour, the Immortal One, Light (I Tim. i. 17; ii. 3; iv. 10; vi. 16; Titus ii 13) reflects Hellenistic cultic terminology as does the use of 'appearing' for Christ's incarnation and parousia (I Tim. vi. 14; II Tim. i. 10; Titus ii. 13; cf. II Cor. iv. 10; Col. iii. 4; II Thess. ii. 8; I Pet. v. 4; I John ii. 28; iii. 2). Behm and Guthrie, who examine the doctrinal question in some detail, rightly emphasize that the terms used cannot be divorced from the subject-matter and purpose of the letters (e.g., combating Gnostic influences) . As Colossians and Ephesians show, this would not be the first time that Paul had turned the religious vocabulary of his opponents against them. If the Pastorals speak of the Law as good (I Tim i. 8; cf. Rom. vii. 12 ff.) or stress good

---

[30] Scott, *op. cit.*, p. xxx.
[31] J. A. T. Robinson, *The Body* (London, 1952), p. 10.

works (I Tim. ii. 10; v. 10; II Tim. ii. 21; iii. 17; Titus ii. 14; cf. Rom. ii. 7; II Cor. v. 10; ix. 8; Eph. ii. 10; vi. 8; Col. i. 10; iii. 23 ff.; II Thess. ii. 17) or equate faith with orthodox doctrine (I Tim. iii. 9; iv. 1, 6; v. 8; II Tim. iii. 8; Titus i. 13; cf. Rom. xvi. 17; Gal. i. 23; Eph. iv. 5; Phil. i. 27; Col. ii. 7) or stress the preservation of tradition (I Tim. vi. 20; II Tim. i. 12, 14; ii. 2; cf. I Cor. xi. 2, 23; xv. 3; II Thess. ii. 15; iii. 6), they may not be entirely in accord with emphases of the other Paulines; but neither is there an incredible contrast. In attempting to restrict genuine Pauline thought patterns to the emphases of the *Hauptbriefe* we may be influenced more than we realize by the ghosts of the Tübingen School. Certainly, good works are viewed not as in the later 'merit' theology but, as in Paul, to show forth the genuineness of one's faith (cf. II Tim. i. 9; Titus iii. 5; cf. also II Tim. ii. 19 with Phil. ii. 12 f). The Pauline concept of faith as trust or belief is also present (cf. I Tim. i. 5, 14; ii. 15; cf. Col. i. 23; II Tim. i. 5; iii. 15); and although the Holy Spirit is mentioned only infrequently, he is named in Colossians (i. 8) and II Thessalonians (ii. 13) only once and in Philemon not at all. All in all, the problem of theological peculiarities may be stated in one question: Are the divergencies so great that they cannot reasonably be explained as the product of the mind of Paul? Perhaps the balance of authority still answers yes. There is, however, a growing negative opinion which is persuaded otherwise.

There are problems involved in accepting the Pauline authorship of the Pastoral epistles. Within the framework of a 'secretary hypothesis' some of these are alleviated, although variations in theological emphasis and expression remain. On the other hand one wonders if the advocates of the 'fragment theory' and the 'later Paulinist theory', in dethroning the tradition, have fully faced the problems besetting their own views.[32] It is difficult to understand why the Pastorals should be so superior to other second-century pseudepigrapha. What motivated just these letters of just this type to just these recipients? If from Pauline fragments, how and why were the fragments preserved? — they appear to have no coherence. How could such a hodgepodge be so smoothly integrated into the letters that even now there is no agreed identification of the fragments? Is there any parallel elsewhere in the patristic Church for fragments being so utilized? What is the genius of the Paulinist which enables him to portray so precisely the psychological traits of advancing age?[33] Hypothetical answers to these questions come easily — perhaps too easily. For many inquirers the questions remain unanswered.

A final problem for those rejecting the Pastorals is the question of pseudepigrapha itself. One cannot, of course, place any blanket condemnation over pseudepigrapha as an improper literary form. But Torm, one of the few writing at length on this question, reminds us that the question cannot be ignored. Certainly a 'pious fraud', produced to invoke apostolic authority upon the views of a later writer, raises ethical questions; fragments gathered and expanded to express the apostle's thought would be nearer the line of ethical propriety. The deposing of the Asian elder for his innocent romance of *Paul*

---

32 Cf. Guthrie, *op. cit.*, pp. 23 f., 44, 49 ff.
33 Cf. C. Spicq, *Les épitres pastorales* (Paris, 1947), pp. lxxxix ff.

and Thecla, the emphasis upon apostolicity as a test for canonicity, and the mass of rejected 'apocryphal New Testament' literature suggest that the patristic Church was not nearly so bland towards the ethics of pseudepigrapha as some modern writers have supposed. Any final conclusion that the Pastorals are pseudonymous must face anew the propriety of their canonicity. This is not an improper question; in fact, as Professor Filson admonishes us,[34] it is always the Church's duty to re-examine its heritage. But it is not a question that those rejecting Pauline authorship can lightly dismiss or brush aside.

It is not likely that the question of authorship of the Pastorals will find a unanimous answer in the near future. Among those favouring their genuineness are scholars representing a considerable variation of theological viewpoint: Zahn (1906), Torm (1932), Thoernell (1933), Schlatter (1936), Michaelis (1946), Spicq (1947), Behm (1948), de Zwaan (1948), Jeremias (1953), Simpson (1954), and Guthrie (1957). For a minority report this roster is not unimpressive and, if a conjecture is to be made, it may be that the future trend will lie in their direction.

[34] F. V. Filson, *Which Books Belong in the Bible?* (Philadelphia, 1957), pp. 131 ff.

INDEX OF REFERENCES
OLD TESTAMENT

NEW TESTAMENT

EXTRA-CANONICAL